On the Shoulders of Mighty Women

*A Modern Feminist's Guide to an Equitable,
Diverse World*

*For Mitzi,
With love and
gratitude,
Lesley Michaels*

by
Lesley Michaels

On The Shoulders of Mighty Women

Copyright © 2022 Lesley Michaels

Lesley Michaels

Boston, MA

Team@LesleyMichaels.com

Ordering Information:

Special discounts are available on quantity purchases by corporations, associations, educational institutions, and others. For details, contact Lesley Michaels above.

Printed in the United States of America

First Edition

Hardcover ISBN 978-1-5136-9377-4

Softcover ISBN 978-1-5136-9378-1

eBook ISBN 978-1-5136-9392-7

Library of Congress 2022939946

Publisher

Winsome Entertainment Group LLC

TESTIMONIALS

"Lesley Michaels brings a wealth of knowledge, experience, humanity and wisdom to the issue of how women can and should support each other. She blends personal experience and the latest in brain science, with that rare and beautiful quality, agape, unselfish concern for the welfare of others. She is one of the Mighty Women she writes about!"

Mitzi Perdue (Mrs. Frank Perdue), Speaker, Business-Woman and Author of a Mark Victor Hansen biography (the Chicken Soup for the Soul guy)

"On the Shoulders of Mighty Women is a provocative, gutsy call to women to set down all lingering ideas of smallness and stand as the 'Mighty Women' they truly are."

Precious Williams, Bestselling Author of The Pitch Queen, A Woman's Journey From Poverty to Purpose & Profits

"Lesley Michaels celebrates women with grit, humor, and love. She is the unicorn that she mentions in On the Shoulders of Mighty Women, and we are all better off for her magic."

Betsy Gaines Quammen, PhD, Bestselling Author of American Zion

"Building alliances, leaning into resilience, and finding true empowerment are just a few of the monumental topics tackled in On the Shoulders of Mighty Women. A must read!"

Adam Markel, Bestselling Author of Change Proof

"Lesley Michaels is a seasoned professional whose insights about women and empowerment soar above most. I highly recommend this book for women who want to break the cultural confines passed down by an oppressive patriarchal society. This is your time. This book encourages you to emerge into your true self and to break the chains that bind your imagination, creativity, and power."

Anne Sermons Gillis, MS, Interspiritual Minister, Author

"The powerful vulnerability, the rich spectrum of shared wisdom and knowledge, and the remarkable storytelling contained in On the Shoulders of Mighty Women is high fidelity GPS for navigating in these challenging times of reassessment and evolution with courage and compassion. Lesley Michaels has written the book we all need right now, women and men alike, and, as the mighty woman she is, has offered us her own shoulders upon which to stand."

Sandra Bargman, Actor, Author, Influencer

"I highly recommend On the Shoulders of Mighty Women. This is a book of empowerment. It provides a road map for moving beyond fear, breaking through societal norms, challenging negative thoughts and behaviors, while celebrating the true you. Lesley Michaels uses case studies and brain science to illustrate why we do what we do and how we can grow and change. Be prepared to step into your excellence!"

Lisa Charles, Author, Speaker and Transformational Coach

"Lesley Michaels hits the mark with this insightful look into the undercurrents of envy, jealousy, and incivility in the modern-day workspace. Companies that wish to flourish should buy copies of her book and give it to all executives as required reading. It is high time that we, as women, step out in kindness, speaking the truth, with the intention to uplift each other."

Angela Legh, Author

"On the Shoulders of Mighty Women is one of those illuminating read one, share one books that speaks such straightforward truths that it changes the way we see ourselves and the world around us."

Dr. Angelika Maria Koch, Doctor of Natural Medicine, Author

"Lesley brings to light an invaluable topic: trust. Trust is earned. Never given. For all of us, including future generations. Lesley's piece of literature is yet another "must" for all self-developers, no matter their walk of life."

Daisy Papp, Author, The Island Model

To the power and grace of those women who came before,
the ones who will follow,
the warriors and the fallen.

FOREWARD

You know the moment you meet someone who seemingly can see into your soul? Someone who understands and so eloquently affirms your thoughts and experiences in ways that surprise you?

In that moment, you think to yourself, "I wish I met her 15 years ago!"

Those were the words crystallized in my mind when I met Lesley Michaels, the author and guide for the incredible journey you are about to take.

I'd just launched my book, "Infinitely More. Choosing Freedom, A Career Mom's Turning Point." It's a story behind the surveys of why women leave big jobs and how leaders lose them. It's my story and, as I'd learn, the story of so many women who pivoted during the COVID-19 pandemic – and beyond.

I knew I wasn't "alone" in my career experiences. Yet, there I was feeling alone as I stood up to share what so many endure but can't say aloud about workplace inequities. As tough as I am, embracing this taboo subject was as scary and intimidating as it gets. It was the first time I'd been willing to acknowledge publicly systemic inequities that hold women back in ways still not fully appreciated or understood, no matter our industry or profession.

As fate would have it, shortly after the launch, I'd been asked to join Lesley on her podcast, "Women We Should Know." Preparing to meet her, I was nervous. My palms were sweaty. Jittery. Of course, I'd done my homework. I knew about Lesley's extraordinary experiences as a businesswoman, her reputation as an internationally known speaker and gifted writer, and her expertise in building strategic alliances.

Yet what moved me most was that Lesley is and has always been a woman ahead of her time. An ardent supporter of women and outspoken advocate for equality and equity for decades, she seemed to tackle these hard conversations with ease. Worldly and

VII

wise. Direct and strategic. Poised and gracious. Lesley has interviewed and collaborated with countless, well-known – even famous – women. And me? I was just getting started. A newbie to this scene. I had much to learn.

I don't get intimidated easily. A former prosecutor and a corporate investigations and crisis management lawyer for decades, I'm used to excavating and dissecting hard topics. I'm skilled at tough conversations and navigating thorny issues. Yet, there I was. A pile of nerves. Lesley could see right through me.

As you'll soon see for yourself and true to her nature, Lesley has a gift for melting fear away and putting people at ease. With her combination of old school charm and hardcore realism, she's a master at building connections and making a lone soul feel like she's part of an army. She disarms her subjects with her wit and curiosity. She has an uncanny ability to lull you into feeling safe. It's like you're sitting at her kitchen table, soaking in the afternoon sun reflecting from her windows, music playing softly in the background, and drinking a warm cup of tea – all the while sharing stories, tackling hard topics, affirming emotions, exchanging ideas, and opening your eyes to real world challenges, possibility, and hope. And, yes, she even offers concrete tools to make more serious progress on equality and equity for all women.

That's right. Even amidst the feelings of chaos and fear, Lesley offers the impossible.

Possibility. Hope. Practical advice.

Lesley is a special brew of warmth, harsh realism, and genuine optimism.

I was truly honored, humbled, and secretly in awe when Lesley asked me to write the Foreward to this incredible book. For one thing, it assured I would have the grand opportunity to read "On the Shoulders of Mighty Women" before its release. More importantly though, I got an early peek at lessons and answers I'd yearned for. An advocate and problem-solver by nature, I was looking for answers and wisdom from women who forged these thorny pathways before me.

Lesley does not disappoint. Filled with rich storytelling, pointed lessons learned, and intriguing ideas for rebuilding alliances for the future, this book is filled with reflections and advice that force us to pause, think, cheer, and read passages again. Lesley pulls no punches in taking on the role we each play in the equity game, men and women – but especially women. After all, it is up to women to honor their innate powers, to join forces to champion and mentor each other and, above all, to reject scarcity of opportunity by aligning together and refusing to turn our sisters into competitive enemies.

Lesley is unapologetic in her love and respect for women, no matter their career or life choices. More than anyone, she deeply understands and honors the burdens we carry, the impossible choices we must make in relationships and motherhood, and the tricky issues we face in our careers and life. As the pages unfold, she leaves room for every possible feeling in a woman's journey from nostalgia and joy to sadness and anger to utter frustration and celebration. Yet, she always returns to hope, realism - and a multifaceted plan to tackle existing barriers.

"On the Shoulders of Mighty Women" honors where the mighty women of today came from while shining a light on where we might go from here. This book is not just about honoring mighty women of the past and present, it is about encouraging and empowering mighty women of the future to take their rightful, storied places among their older sisters, mothers, and grandmothers. Those mighty women upon whose shoulders younger generations soon will climb.

Lesley shows that none of us are alone in our journeys unless we choose to be. That alone is a most gratifying truth. She invites us to join forces, extend hands, and stand tall.

Now, if you are ready, I invite you to gather pen and paper by your side as you sink into a soft chair and immerse yourself in the pages that follow. For this is not just a book to be read. It is a book to absorb for those looking to the future.

I hope you relish in its wisdom.

~ *Amy Conway-Hatcher*
Advocate, author of Infinitely More

Introduction

When I close my eyes and imagine in vivid detail the first time I experienced permission to create my own definitions in life, in business, as a woman - it was bittersweet. I'd imagined each success I'd known up to that moment as being shaped by my own choosing. In an instant I recognized them as having been rooted in other people's ideas, unknowingly adopted. The shroud of insecurities well seeded during my youth had left me incapable of such a bold move as to grant myself permission. But this moment, this moment was different, defining. At the time, I was working on a new initiative and had noticed I was running into an emotional roadblock each time I tried to expand into it. Anyone dealing in intellectual work understands how frustrating this can be and how quickly this kind of internal brick wall can derail a project.

It was a gentle evening. A friend was over for dinner, and we were laughing as Bob Marley filled the space between every wall. Warm from a glass of tempranillo and dancing to Reggae, I began to notice the most surreal sensation overtaking me, saturating every sense. It felt like unreserved happiness but subdued in an internal kind of way. This stirring from deep within washed over and through my entire existence like a knowing of something transparently obvious. How could I have never seen, felt or known this before? A sensation of calm and sure knowing filled every cell. At the center of this wave rested a visceral absence of all doubt. In that moment I knew that I had stumbled into the access point for my own visions, the internal doorway for living from my own knowing. It was a sensation of deep expansion like I'd never imagined. Far more potent was the awareness of my capacity to serve, from hard-fought wisdom I hadn't until that moment dared to call mine, dared to internalize. Permission to walk away from tradition and follow my own insight, clarity, daring and to make my own choices finally belonged to me, and at long last I felt enough to claim that space. But this wasn't the first time I'd experienced a dream of living the life of a free woman.

Sheltered by the shade of the giant tree in my parent's front yard, I was deep in focus, busily scribbling notes as quickly as my hand would travel the paper. I'd had a dream, one so deep and true that the sensation and vision of the heat of that day, my cut-off shorts and little white cotton shirt with its red piping can still travel from that 12-year-old moment, into this current time.

The dream to bring women together to uplift one another had been born and continued to periodically revisit throughout the years, only to again fade into the recesses of my mind. At 59 I noticed how increasing numbers of women in their 30's, 40's and even some in their 50's were stepping up to do this very thing. I felt forced to contemplate the obvious. Somewhere along the road I had driven right past the corner, missing that all important turn in my life's path. Then, one day, while in the shower the words came as clearly as if someone had been physically speaking. "It's never too late." Inexplicable as it may sound, there was no doubt this was my long-held vision revealing it's time had come.

Reflection took over, of how long I'd waited to give myself this gift of trusting the dream and my ability to give it a life of its own. The financial, emotional, psychic states of abject poverty of safety, security and the basic needs of life that had haunted each day of my formative years had taken their rightful place. In the past. Pivoting into what felt like the next natural step of my own womanhood and success allowed me to plant my feet on solid ground, no longer sinking into the quicksand that had pulled me under during my early introduction to life, business, and being female.

Womanhood can present us with a double-edged sword or stand representative of endless choice. While this can all simultaneously be true, my many trips around the sun have taught me something I don't hear many women talk about. Womanhood can present us with a double-edged sword, or stand representative of endless choice. It is the entire potential the Universe has to offer, from giving life to running a Fortune 500; from partnering with a beloved to favoring singledom.

As women, we are taught to be meager, small in our space, and 'nice'. So the power available within choice itself can present as a discomfort many women work tirelessly to avoid. For those with the courage to never surrender to the status quo, a switch flips and understanding begins to dawn - this is no sword, single or double-edged. Not at all. When activated, choice has the potential to be our victory cry, our superpower, the reminder of one simple yet very profound truth: women can do anything.

As we overcome that sometimes mountainous terrain threatening to stop us in our tracks, choice becomes our window into realizing there is no limitation to how we fill our lives. The time has come that we honor our anger. The time has come that we honor our fear. The time has come that we honor our emotions, our vulnerability, our guilt and our shame. The time has come that we allow our capacity to lead us directly into the center of our greatest presence as Women. The time has come that we make space for ourselves and our inherent genius. This is the moment to shrug the weight of the world off of our shoulders, as so many mighty women have, for eons before. The moment is here for setting down the burden of what we've been taught about womanhood and cease to pass it forward to our daughters and younger sisters, as the most unkind gift we could possibly offer.

The women before you and I created space for us at a breadth to which they had not possessed access. The legacy they left is simple: create your own space and own it. Lean into your womanhood. Celebrate your potential. Acknowledge that you've had the power to do so all along, and you will never let fear or anger or labels or expectations stop you - ever again. The most compelling admonishment within our female ancestors bequeathment cautions; Never use your power or access to space to stop another woman, no matter her path, or where she happens to be upon it.

Historical feminism and the evolution of women's freedom represents another simple truth: our external fight to actualize the choices to which we've inherently known we had a right. We've known, collectively, how much we were, are and have been capable of. We've known, collectively, how much the weight of the world rests on the shoulders of females/women/mothers/sisters. Women are not the rightful weight bearers for the entirety of humanity. Our lives are ours to own, to explore, and to live. A concept many women struggle to demand out of the guilt, shame, and fear that we are told we deserve, that we are forced to swallow.

We've known, collectively, that we were always due an equitable playing field and yet it continues to elude us. This being partially due to a different application of a woman's sword. The one in which it is women wielding their sharp blades against other women. An experience I became familiar with during my tenure as one of the early women thrust into the corporate world of oil and gas.

The ruthless competitiveness of the women I encountered in that environment was both shocking and emotionally fracturing. I'd been weaned on feminist ideology by an audacious paternal suffragette/grandmother. My teens found me in NYC during the height of the Women's Liberation Movement. Women were joined in the push for the Equal Rights Amendment. A few short years later, the foreignness of these corporate women's approach to other women was inconceivable and convinced me to abandon that world, altogether.

I was confused. I thought women were each other's strength, advocates, inspiration and that they held a unified focus of lifting each other on their mighty shoulders. More years of ebb and flow in business taught me how wrong I was. Yes, women were...are... strong enough to hold the entire world and all other women on their shoulders. But at what point had each woman along the way become weary of the weight on their round shoulders, and started to project their frustration onto other women? How are we to collectively claim equity status when so many among our numbers are acting as great oppressors to others of us?

As a third-generation feminist, I feel called to expose this flaw, clearly disrupting the entire system. The one where women who have found their space believe there is not enough room to dare to include other women. What level of generational fear were they carrying, are we carrying, that compels us to viciously guard space that has the capacity to expand outward exponentially? At what point do we accept the most fruitful truth of them all, which is that women can do anything. No matter how many of us there are, no matter how far we go, no matter what our dreams are - no matter what. If you want to ostracize me because I've chosen differently than you, you're cheating yourself of the equity attainable through feminism. Should I wish to take the oil industry by the horns, so to speak, and make a fortune doing it, should matter no less or no more than if I decide to homeschool four children and live on a self-sustaining farm.

Have you ever found yourself stepping back from an opportunity because you felt small when looking at the others participating? Or have you declined invitations because you couldn't feel the potential the one making the offer saw in you? Have you heard the saying, "You are YOU and that is your superpower?" We forget how much we are capable of, lock away our potential, compare ourselves to others who simply are not us, and then wonder how life got away from us.

The difficulty rests in our hesitancy to make a choice from the vast potential that can either imprison or free us. Every day we inch closer to exercising our voices, to truly choosing how we will fill our time, occupy our freedom, and do so with the same carelessness and worry-free mentality as males around the world... and where will we go from here? Where will we *choose* to go from here? Are we willing to step into our journey as mighty women? Will we grant ourselves permission to recognize our greatness?

Let's build alliance, create great things together, and leave a bolder, richer legacy, with a stake well planted in the ground of equity for those women who will follow. Can we, together, experience womanhood through a new lens, one that has been ignored? One that has been designed throughout the course of our entire history - *on the shoulders of very mighty women.*

Women who do not compete with other women.
Women willing to stand in the fire with their sisters.
Women who build each other up and rise together.
Those women are not just women,
They are Queens.

*~ **Brooke Hampton***

CONTENTS

Part One

Chapter One

"A strong woman stands up for herself. A stronger woman stands up for everybody else."

~ *Anonymous*

A CIRCLE OF WOMEN

My life has been lived in a circle of women and it was they who, early in my youth, set my focus on seeing all people treated with dignity and respect. While those who inflamed my passion did not always bear the same faces or personalities, they were primarily female.

This began with an English mother who spent her early years in WWII bomb shelters. Having watched her mum die in that war when she was only six, she was brought up by her ever-so-proper grandmother. Like so many of the war-traumatized young women of her time, she later married the American she had met only six weeks earlier. Shortly after the nuptials she was whisked away to the post-war fantasies of an idyllic American life. Don't we all know where dreams of idyllic happy-endings lead?

Juxtapose this with an audacious paternal grandmother who exercised her brilliance to emancipate herself, long before the majority of women. With no desire to become a farm wife she put her inherent gift for strategic thinking to work. At fifteen she convinced the young man who had been courting to elope by running away to another state. Her best friend, who was the bank owner's daughter, became her champion and advocate. As they ignored the numerous laws of the age that forbade such *heresies,* my grandmother came to own her own home and her own business, in her own name, by the early 1940's.

In reflection, it is this grandmother's outrageous actions that stand out as my introduction to the idea of women's alliance. She and her friend were my models for what can be achieved when women bond around intentional support of one another. It was her ongoing accomplishments that gave me permission to imagine that women have everything it takes to create an adventurous and successful life, on their own terms.

Long prior to that realization dawning, the divergency offered by these three very different way-showers produced more questions than answers in my young mind, regarding women. Who were they? What were they *supposed* to be? What was their place and role in the world? I was looking for blanket answers and definitions I was too young to imagine, as not existing. Only in retrospect did I recognize the mixed messages of my youth had left me no alternative but to create my own meanings of life. It wasn't until a conversation with my paternal grandmother during her end days, that I came to celebrate the emancipation within this inadvertent gift. She spoke of how deeply satisfying it had been to witness one of her six granddaughters setting down traditional expectations to chart her own course. My grandmother's final great gift was the admonition *"never look back and never let anyone tell you who to be."* The journey for which I had received only this single crib note presented itself as a series of flashes of sureness that would later implode upon themselves. This was mixed up with little insights of authentic clarity that fed me at profound levels and ensured my quest would bear fruit.

By my early teens the broadly sweeping sociological and political messages of the times made life all-the-more confusing. These were the years of transitioning from the black and white world of Leave It to Beaver and Make Room for Daddy into the full-color spectrum of the blossoming hippie movement, the fight for both civil rights and women's rights, protests against the war in Viet Nam and the emergence of a psychedelic nation. Growing up during these progressing eras was equal parts exhilarating and disorienting.

It was a fortunate accident of fate that I was at the younger end of the boomer generation. We were about a minute into the '70's when I was filled with a deep hunger to understand women in broader dimensions than what my three primary influencers had presented. It took an additional number of years to distinguish this as a desire to understand who I was growing into. With beginnings like these, sticking my thumb out and hitchhiking to the east coast, into the heart of the women's movement, was as natural as breathing.

Finding myself surrounded by women working to create something more for the whole of humanity crystalized my fascination with the power of the female spirit. It was an up close and personal window into all that we bring to each other and what can be accomplished by moving *in alliance* toward a common goal. Thus began the formulation of my personal definitions. A quest that lasted decades and, as life will be, was full of potholes counterbalanced with striking recognitions. While the Equal Rights Amendment was not adopted, and all this time later there is still much road to travel in the name of equality and equity, much was accomplished by, for, and among women. The stage had been set for continuing progressions, both personally and globally.

Womanance

While the volume lowered for a time after the Equal Rights Amendment failed to be ratified, women never relinquished the pursuit. During the past few decades, a growing number of females have started to claim their own space in new and potent ways. More women from every demographic are dedicating the time and energy necessary to truly know themselves. With this comes the confidence to create personal interpretations and determine one's own trajectories.

The motivating principles for these daring moves toward autonomy are rooted in the punishing expectations women still encounter. Whether it be directed at them personally or filtered in through our media, from our marketers, by way of the distorted presentations on reality TV, or through ongoing societal challenges, it is a daily experience. One key area centers around appearance; be it beauty, age, proportion, or fashion choice. Then there are the mainstream standards that govern 'correct' management of relationships, career and family. To marry, partner, neither? This is followed by expectations of whether to parent or not to parent. A career or no career? The more grueling oppressions marginalize women for their race, culture, religious allegiance and sexual orientation.

It is to women's benefit that they are inherent bonders. So much so that the new language 'womanance' has been coined to describe close, non-sexual, non-romantic relationships between two or more women. A poignant example arose during a recent Women's Entrepreneurial Alliance Group of which I'm a member. One younger participant was sharing her frustration with why women *have* to work so much harder to listen, hear, and understand everyone around them. Why it is assumed that the women in the room will ensure that everyone else is comfortable, both in general and with her specific presence? Shouldn't each individual be responsible for their own reactions? Having helped her identify the core issue, one of our more seasoned professionals offered a different take on the matter. Speaking of having met another member only 18 months earlier, she shared how she already knows this woman's mind, heart, soul, fears and would fight tigers for her. Addressing the demand on women to be more fully present from this alternate perspective of standing strong with one another, illustrated that we can carry these societal traditions as a burden or amplify it as a superpower.

In recent years, the words women and superpower have been linked so frequently that there are ongoing studies into what this includes. According to some scientific research, all women possess certain superpowers. What qualifies them as such is the lack of these same abilities within the majority of men. In an extended study, Israel Abramov, psychologist and behavioral neuroscientist at CUNY's Brooklyn College, distinguished that women have a physiological ability to more acutely detect the nuance in shades of color. There is untold research indicating that women possess stronger immune systems, resulting in longer life expectancies. Studies from numerous institutes indicate that while stress increases empathic and intuitive abilities in women it undermines the same in men. This explains why further investigation demonstrates women possess enhanced skill for detecting danger. The fact that women can multitask with seeming effortlessness has been long established. This all begs the question, *"how can women use these valuable advantages as springboards for remembering they are far more than they frequently imagine?"*

The Matter of Alliance

I have witnessed little more powerful than groups of women who have set down the weight of patriarchal training to become truly aligned. These relationships stand as potential templates for how we can help each other to discover ourselves, strengthen our skills, hone our talents, and claim a posture of enhanced self-confidence.

There is no denying that great strides will be made as we equalize the gender balance within the boardrooms, C-Suites and through all levels of business. However, this is not the sum and substance of women. A time traveler arriving here in this period and discovering google as a source of all things might find this surprising. The majority of what immediately pops up about women, leadership, and equality is wholly centered on business. To be genuinely seen and understood, to achieve equality and equity throughout our lives, it will be necessary to develop a broad-based commitment to something at which women naturally excel: Collaboration.

While this undoubtedly carries value within the work environment, it is arguably even more important when aligning on issues that extend to our many other responsibilities and concerns in life. From politically motivated agendas and social justice allyship to the many facets of our private lives, women can understand the challenges of each other at a deeply felt level. In one expression or another, we've all been there ourselves. While there are essential reasons for continued learning based on our myriad of race, culture, and sexual orientation, we do understand the multidimensionality of being a woman in this world. When we focus our inherent ability to relate to each other through female collectives we become more than the sum of our parts.

7

The Power Behind Aligning

Where do we begin? One option is reviewing a template based on collaboration between myself and a fantastic group of women, building intentional groups for strategic alliance.

A Women's Alliance can serve many topical purposes. Whatever the specificity of a group the result is an understanding and deeper interpretation of the psychological processes that divide women from one another. This holds true whether a particular group is focused on professional acceleration, social justice or any other area of life. A well-formed Women's Alliance will reveal the social divisions between women in the specific arena of focus. It will help the members become conscious of how they play into the societally trained patterns of competitive disassociation from one another. We each carry internalized oppressions and false value assessments, many of which have been masterfully hidden, to the degree of our lacking any honest recognition of their consequence. How they impact areas of life beyond the obvious is well camouflaged. Participating in thoughtful, focused conversation for a specific purpose can inadvertently lead members toward recognition of self-limiting beliefs that affect their lives in ways they'd never considered. Everyone engaged in the alignment experience, with intention, benefits.

"Alliance is when all stakeholders benefit equally. You're bringing a set of assets, and I'm bringing my own set. We see an equal opportunity to create something that we couldn't do alone," explains Shelmina Abji, empowerment speaker and former IBM Vice President.

Due to all the *good girl* training a female typically experiences during her youth, women tend toward resistance about revealing their imagined shortcomings. So many times I've witnessed how women bringing their voices together from a space of honesty and courageous transparency, produces great forward movement for each. This starts from within as glimmers of recognition of strengths previously not validated. Typically these awarenesses are coupled with the feeling of courage to be more present with the

8

group. The momentum continues to evolve. More of the ties to dated beliefs consistently fall away, thus empowering strategically aligned women in the day-to-day of their lives.

When building a Woman's Alliance Group, a good starting place is identifying women you would like to know better, learn from, share with, and support. Begin having conversations that reveal if the women you are thinking of fit this frame. Ask questions, in a non-interrogative way, about their perspectives on the subject that will be the foundation of your group. Listen empathetically to their responses. Instead of just hearing them, feel what they are sharing. Remember that you don't have to build this by yourself. We all have broad spheres of influence. When there are two to three of you committed to developing a group, each is likely to know women that the others do not. Diversity adds richness to a Women's Alliance. Invite women of different demographics, cultures, races and experiences.

Most significant is remembering that although you have selected an area of group focus, the greatest benefit you will each receive is what you will learn about yourselves. Certainly, you will increase your knowledge about the primary topic and how others handle its impact. However, approaching an alliance from a mindset of openness to learn is the strongest potential enrichment you can offer yourself and the group.

Developing Strategic Alliance Groups

Here are some of my best tips for establishing a Women's Alliance Group:

Choose Your Topic

Being clear about your topic will help the conversations stay on point therein making the meetings a worthy time investment. This will help you identify who might be a good fit for the group. It also lets potential members determine if it's the right fit for them.

A few examples:

- Social Justice (Is there a specific area of focus?)
- Unveiling unconscious bias
- Balancing work/home life
- Women's political action
- Addressing internalized misogyny
- Female solopreneurs
- Female entrepreneurs
- Female small business owners

Assign a Name to the Group

This clarifies your collective intention and gives the group a level of gravitas which reminds members that there is true purpose to the meetings.

Make It a Closed Group

Choose your maximum participants from the onset. Most of us have seen groups on various social media sites with 100's to 1000's of members. While these do serve a valuable purpose, this is not a true Alliance Group. With numbers this large only a few really get to know each other. I've often seen it produce multiple splinter groups, each having only a few people who interact directly. Additionally, the nature of online messaging versus personal conversation all but eliminates the potential for true, heartfelt connection.

It is my recommendation that an alliance group include no more than 12 women. This is a sufficient number to ensure there will always be enough voices in the room to make the time allotment worthwhile. Concurrently, it is small enough to avoid becoming cumbersome when most members are able to attend a single meeting.

Equity

To create a highly successful Alliance Group it is important to ensure that every woman has equity. Invite members to volunteer to lead a meeting with their own content. Sharing in this way is a responsibility, but also an opportunity. Members get to rehearse new content within a group of women who already support them as alliance partners. The end result being that closer bonds naturally develop, because everyone feels equal, included and valued.

Fundamental Points to Address

To achieve what is only possible within an environment known to be *safe*, ask each member to verbally agree to confidentiality.

When you are in the meeting, be 'in' the meeting. No calls, texting, or private Zoom chats. Agree to ask clarifying questions vs telling a member what they *should* do or speaking in corrective tones.

Unconscious Bias Groups

An across-the-board commitment to being willing to agree to disagree when discussing sticking points, while remaining in the 'room', attentively contributing and receiving is essential.

This is deeply necessary with topics like unconscious bias or internalized misogyny. You are there to uncover your own and support each other in doing the same. It is unthinkable that you won't occasionally run into a trigger point.

Professional Based Alliance Groups

A pushback I often encounter when discussing Women's Alliance with females from within the same workplace or industry is, *"How can we support each other when we are pursuing similar goals?"* The Female Quotient's CEO, Shelly Zalis is often quoted as saying, *"There's power in the pack. A woman alone has power; together, we have impact."*

Women's Alliance is an open door to claiming and bolstering that impact. It emboldens us, as a whole, to cease veiling our most effective and powerful selves, either as an act of self-protection or for others comfort. The natural byproduct of more women building intentional alliances, is that we get to see ourselves through a new lens. I have personally found great solace in hearing other women *confess* to self-limiting perceptions that they imagined other's not possessing. Each time I've heard one of my own self-limiting thoughts or beliefs expressed by another woman, I experienced an immediate sense of expanded freedom. In turn, the woman courageously speaking up is reinforced by learning her fear or anxiety is not a personal shortcoming or moral failing. We have so much to offer one another and giving ourselves permission to take the time to engage in alliances provides an environment for discovery.

Chapter Two

"The minute you learn to love yourself you won't want to be anyone else"

~ *Rihanna*

FRIENDING YOURSELF

The importance of well-honed communication skills for developing successful relationships can't be overstated. What is discussed less frequently is how this applies to the communications we have with ourselves, formally termed "intrapersonal communication". This is not a reference to the mental diatribes we can inflict upon ourselves for even the slightest misdemeanor. Rather it applies to the expressions of communication that let us understand ourselves, learn new things and problem solve. Who of us hasn't had lengthy internal discussions when breaking a problem down into bite-sized pieces or developing a new strategy? Yet conversations with ourselves extend beyond these valuable exercises. A notable percentage of our intrapersonal communications are rooted in the negative self-images we carry. They may be founded in self-judgments that started as negative projections from others. Then there are the denouncements we've created through comparison to some externalized ideal. Whatever the genesis of an undermining intrapersonal communication, the results are similarly destructive and isolating.

Communication as a means of relating to another did not exist in the home in which I grew up. Yelling, silent treatments, accusations, and an unrelenting cloud of fear were the norm. Communication was not part of the mix. The fear was top-down. For their individual and joint reasons, both parents spent the majority of their days oozing this energy all over everyone within proximity. Consequently, it was a rare occasion when someone outside the family dared to enter, or for that matter, was invited.

The hostility of the environment successfully pounded into me an assurance that I was born with some indefinable yet unforgivable flaw.

Having taught myself to read by age three, books became my solitary refuge, my singular *safe* friend. I've reaped many benefits from the years I spent buried in their pages, hiding away in my self-imposed isolation. The list of what they taught me is quite simply, endless. From early on we lacked the financial fluidity to buy books. So, every Saturday morning my mother would load us up in her Vista Cruiser station wagon and off to the library we'd go. I always returned with as many books as I could possibly stuff into my brown grocery bag, without bursting its sides. I was set for another week. Our single indulgence was the purchase of a full set of Encyclopedia Britannica. By the time I was twelve I'd flipped through their thick, satiny pages, reading each one cover to cover so many times I simply couldn't bear to pick them up any longer.

As much as I loved those literary friends, there was always a nagging hunger for something more rumbling in my gut. Their facts and stories couldn't fill the deep and ever-present loneliness that haunted me. Even later, when I was independent, neither my passion for books nor the unquieting loneliness abated. This presented the ultimate juxtaposition. I needed to hide so that no one would discover my absolute wrongness and I was lonely and thirsting to know and understand the people I personally encountered as clearly as I did the ones from my literature. I don't know if I was born hungry for people and the isolation of my youth fed into what became my passion. Maybe it was born of those first 7-8 years. Either way, the fascination to know who people were, what they were, why they were, stayed with me, becoming a primary theme of my adult life. Before I could get close to them, I had to make peace with myself and quell the internal war my childhood had set into motion.

For years when people would offer wonderful compliments about who I was, my immediate response was to put my foot in it to prove to them what they didn't understand; that I was not who they had mistaken me for being. I worked to present as the person I'd been taught to think I was. Never did I lend consideration to the idea that I had a choice. It felt like a matter of *what is, is*. I spent a few decades trying to un-become that horrible person before happening upon the simple notion that everything I believed about myself was based on false premises. That enjoyable person people had mistaken me for did exist in there, *somewhere*.

This realization reset my focus in the direction of a great quest. I was going to find that woman who had been long buried under the rubble. I was ready to unload the debris her unevolved self had taken on and jealously protected. Some naïve part of me thought that realization alone was going to quickly propel me to discovery of some long-hidden truth. Instead, it was an extended trek of one micro-step after another. The first glimmer of hope arrived as I recognized that I had no clue what flipped on my inner light switch. It was fascinating to discover I was not alone in this. Along the road, I encountered many women who could list any number of things they enjoyed, but none that set them on fire. Instead, these activities and engagements fell under the heading of things they were expected to do, enjoy, or find fulfilling.

They already felt lacking. To admit that these 'supposed to's' weren't the end all, be all, they had been touted to be would have only made them feel worse about themselves. They loved their partners and children. Caring for their elders was second nature, and never something they would have rejected. Some even had careers of which they were fond. But none of those things triggered the inner light to shine or filled them with a sense of vibrance. They didn't awaken each day excited to jump out of bed and get going.

Another unifying discovery was how many women I spoke with who had never noticed the spark was missing. Others had felt the hole in their gut but were afraid to consider what truth that gap might reveal. I could easily relate to this, having only recently happened upon my own gapping inner cavity. If we give voice to it, then what? Pretending not to notice or sidestepping any action are both exercises in avoidance. Each are further self-abuses that affect mental, physical, emotional, and psychic health. They serve as critical barriers to giving ourselves the personal/private moments essential to knowing who we truly are. The unique gift that only we can bring to our own lives as well as that of our families and the greater world remains unrealized. As I discovered all-to-clearly, we can end up feeling lost beyond redemption.

Discovering what lights us up requires engaging with our most sacredly personal selves. This is the pathway from which we can set ourselves free. Becoming willing to be courageously truthful with ourselves opens the trapdoor we have kept tightly locked.

Schedule Me-Time in Your Datebook—Regularly

Work, kids, partner, home, extended family and church, our personal needs or spiritual obligations fill many-a-woman's datebook to the point of squeezing into the margins. Beyond basic maintenance such as dentist, hair stylist, gym, and maybe an occasional massage, women are finding little to no room for themselves. While I never had kids and the majority of my life has been spent single, "no time for me" was my most frequently played song. Prioritizing ourselves by scheduling time for enriching experiences is natural for those who value themselves strongly. As is true for many women, I was skilled at keeping myself too busy to have time for the simple pleasures of life. Things as normal as vacations were beyond the scope of what I was equipped to give myself. This was more than I subconsciously believed I deserved. Very few women I've spoken with are comfortable acknowledging that this behavior is a statement of their perceived self-worth. They speak of their business with obvious pride. They work to maintain the belief that it is their inherent importance that requires them to remain ever busy. Others will tell the old story with authoritative conviction, all-the-while fully aware that it is nothing more than a well-established avoidance mechanism. Both are derailments of self.

I spent the majority of my adult years too busy to live my life; too busy to be seen or heard or recognized because I was convinced I wasn't good enough. This is a basic expression of self-denial. It dims our inner light to the point that we can't feel it internally. Therefore, it can't shine externally. Here's the all-important catch

I discovered through trial and error. Learning to let that light shine requires more than a random minute here and there. It begs true attunement to inner communication. Is the body tired? Is it asking for a massage, an afternoon by the water, drinks, and dinner with good company? Has the mind started to rebel, forgetting things, losing the keys four times a week? Is your body screaming for meditation time, an evening of sitting back in your favorite chair and listening to music? These are all expressions of intrapersonal communication. The more interested we become in listening and then acting on what we hear, the more we learn to value ourselves. That valuing will naturally displace the negative self-perceptions that have had their day.

Having a clear starting place is supremely helpful. The following are practices from the roadmap I created for myself, over time. I have since passed these on to many women who have used them to their own great advantage.

A To-Do List for Me

Using a legal pad will allow you to easily remove the pages for posting in the way I'll explain in a moment. Or, if you happen to have a spare white board, all the better.

Turning your writing surface to the landscape position, draw two vertical lines the full length, separating your writing surface into three columns.

Step 1:

Consider *time, energy* and *financial investment* with each of these questions. Be specific while not overly detailed.

Step 2:

Having listed your to-do's, write a *do by* date beside each item in all three columns.

See Table 1: Three Small on page 19

See Table 2: Two Medium on page 20

See Table 3: One Large on page 20

This chart will become an essential tool in helping you stay on track with keeping your promises to yourself. Maybe the big thing in column 3 is a trip that will require 12-14-18 months of planning. By identifying a date, you can track what steps need to be taken each month along the way. Before you know it, you'll be on that wonderful vacation.

Not committing to a clear and specific date by which you will fulfill one of the promises you made is a different type of promise. One that assures you will betray yourself, yet again.

Display your *To-Do for Me* list or white board in a prominent place that will catch your attention, daily. Your dressing room is an ideal spot as you can develop a ritual of reading it each morning as you get ready for your day. Taking a few minutes with it again at the end of the day when changing into 'around the house' clothes will further reinforce your commitment to the promises you made to yourself, and *are now* keeping.

Making and executing commitments to ourselves is a strategically powerful move toward shifting from living as who we were told we were, to rising as our brilliantly audacious selves. This is how we become an alliance partner to ourselves. It starts at home. Females are taught from early days that everyone surrounding us must come first. If there happens to occasionally be time, energy or attention left over, we can take these meager scraps for ourselves. This is counter to all that is true. If we don't feed ourselves first, we become depleted and have nothing to give to others. The majority of women are well patterned to ignore when this is happening. The entire time red flags are flapping in the breeze, attempting to get our attention. We become grouchy, snappy, laugh infrequently, and only lightly. Anxiety can be a regular companion. We sleep restlessly and wake up only after the third cup of coffee. Actually, fulfilling your To-Do For Me List, one commitment at a time, can produce great resets to old mindsets. Not to mention all the new fun you'll be having.

Table 1: A To-Do for Me List
Three Small

THREE SMALL - What are three small things you never do for yourself but frequently talk about getting around to?

	TIME	ENERGY	FINANCIAL INVESTMENT
SMALL 1			
	Date:	Date:	Date:
SMALL 2			
	Date:	Date:	Date:
SMALL 3			
	Date:	Date:	Date:

Table 2: A To-Do for Me List
Two Medium

TWO MEDIUM - What are two medium size new things you have longed to give yourself but have not yet allowed?

	TIME	ENERGY	FINANCIAL INVESTMENT
MEDIUM 1			
	Date:	Date:	Date:
MEDIUM 2			
	Date:	Date:	Date:

Table 3: A To-Do for Me List
One Large

ONE LARGE - What is one of the big, new things you have always wanted to experience? That thing that you always tuck away as soon as it comes up, deciding it's just not possible.

	TIME	ENERGY	FINANCIAL INVESTMENT
LARGE 1			
	Date:	Date:	Date:

Stop Asking Permission

There's a difference between asking permission and discussing something with a partner to see if both feel it's a choice that will serve the professional or personal relationship. One is expressed by equals while the other demonstrates a position of subservience.

A woman who does not know her value and has not cultivated self-confidence, will continuously seek permission for the right to have her own opinion or preference. Psychologically, physiologically, and sociologically this pattern dates to a time not so long ago when females were property. Owned by their father until married when her husband assumed legal ownership. A thread of this remains within our DNA and the 'right' circumstances can trigger it into action. Then there are the influences of childhood. Particularly when raised by people who were not prepared to parent, and possibly shouldn't have done so. Self-confidence is something that must be cultivated. The fortunate are taught how to develop comfort in their skin from an early age. However, there are far greater numbers of women who find themselves struggling to establish this during their adult years.

The first hurdle is identifying the self-diminishing habit of permission seeking. In most instances it will not be one expressed only with a partner, business associate or intimate. In the absence of self-esteem lives the constant fear of not getting something right, not knowing, not being enough. Everywhere one is engaged in interaction there are opportunities to feel the 'not's'. This leads to permission seeking in order to make our mis-steps smaller or if possible, avoid them altogether. But permission seeking as an adult only serves to restrict self-image.

Over the years I started to notice my active resistance to imagining that I possessed any true self-value. Since taking the proactive stance of owning my talents, skills, and basic human goodness, I've recognized my former behavior patterns in more women than I can track. Women often become embarrassed with realizing they are several decades into life and still asking permission the way children do. They think of it as an inherent character flaw, when in fact it is just a *habit* that was taught at a time when the brain was still malleable and absorbing everything sent its way.

Cambridge Dictionary defines *habit* as:

> *"Something that you do often and regularly without knowing that you are doing it"*

Merriam-Webster Dictionary says:

> *"An acquired mode of behavior that has become nearly or completely involuntary. A settled tendency of behavior."*

These definitions speak to how anyone can exhibit a pattern without realizing they are doing so. Additionally, it explains why women can feel humiliated when they finally notice. It is a pattern of childhood that was not left behind, rather it remained unnoticed in its continuation. Permission seeking is not, in and of itself, the issue. It's a symptom of something far more crippling. A lack of belief in our intelligence, creativity, our intrinsic value beyond caretaking, and so much more. The habit has played out for so long that it is tempting to imagine that eliminating it requires starting from scratch, in developing positive traits. While our habits may not be tuned to their most harmonious rhythm, they've always been within us. Acknowledging them is the very movement that will start to free us from the cycle of self-minimization. Additionally, we have been continuing through our lives and have learned a lot more than what we often give ourselves credit for. Refocusing our attention toward those wonderful traits we have developed along the way, makes letting go of the self-diminishing habit all the easier.

So how do we accomplish this? It all starts with noticing. And not just the words that come with asking for another's approval. Notice the feelings that rise in a challenging or unsettled moment. Walk away for five minutes or a day. Take time with yourself to ask what *you* want. Does it feel like a sound choice? What makes it so? Are there *legitimate* pitfalls you may have not considered? Are you willing to step up for yourself and share the overview of the situation? Are you willing to let someone disagree with your perspective without making yourself wrong? This is one of the biggest challenges for permission seekers. The deficits in their confidence will always trigger them to self-abase for being so terribly wrong, when it may have been someone simply sharing a different vision. The permission seeker hasn't built a solid footing of being able to agree to disagree without the necessity of there being a winner and a loser. Giving yourself the time to feel into a choice before presenting it, can help to buffer against your own condemnation if your plan or idea isn't met with applause.

For women who weren't given the gift of being shown their worth during their youth, this can feel like always being three steps behind everyone else. Each time you take the space to breathe instead of seeking permission, congratulate yourself for claiming your own voice and choice, one step at a time. And be gentle. This is a marathon. Not a sprint.

Build your white board. Practice keeping promises to yourself. Make time for what you want. Live. Don't just move through life. Live it. Give yourself the gift of time with yourself. When there is a choice to be made, pause, and get clear about which direction you honestly prefer. And remember to place yourself in the equation every time you make a choice that involves others. We are each an inextinguishable light. Give *yourself* permission to remove the dark shade that has been muting your brilliance. Grant yourself the authority to become the greatest alliance partner you could imagine.

Introducing Five Modern-day Mighty Women

Over the past number of years I have had the privilege and pleasure of meeting and aligning with a number of modern-day mighty women. Each is reaching out in their own way and area of expertise to share their knowledge, strength and courage with other women around the world. Five of these audacious leaders have generously contributed the second half to the chapter in this book that speaks to their area of expertise.

Modern-day Mighty Woman: Annabel Ascher

Annabel Ascher is a writer, fine art photographer and social activist. At present she is also the Editor-in-Chief and publisher of Taos Magazine, a regional arts magazine for Northern New Mexico.

Making Friends with Myself

There are two old sayings about love that are mistaken. First is "no one can love you if you don't love yourself". And its corollary, "If you don't love yourself, no one can love you". As a person who came very late to loving myself, I know both of these sayings to be incomplete.

I know from experience that we who don't love ourselves can be absolutely devoted to certain other people, usually those who don't love us either. And others can love us deeply, but we won't see it or feel it.

But devotion is not exactly the same as love. We attract those who mirror our degree of self-love.

Friendship

What is friendship? How do we treat our friends? There must be mutual trust, respect, care, and consideration. We want the best for our friends. We listen to them when they are speaking and speak kindly to them in return. We think the best of them and give the benefit of the doubt if we think they messed up. When they celebrate, we celebrate with them, and when they grieve, we do the same.

Then there are the things we don't do. We don't steer them wrong or lie to them or cheat them. We don't put them down and chip away at their self- esteem. We don't gossip about them or speak ill of them behind their backs. We don't sabotage them or abandon them in their time of need.

I was always able to be a good friend to my friends. I understood the give and take, and some of them have been in my life for over

50 years. But there was one person closer than all the rest whom I did not treat like a friend, at least not until very recently. Myself.

Learning Self-Mistrust

My parents were brilliant and moneyed, but also deeply flawed. They liked to blame any deficiencies they were willing to acknowledge on the times. "Things were crazy in the 1960s don't you know..." But it was really them. There were six daughters, and I was number three and the designated scapegoat. They really were not fit to have children at all, but it was what was done at that time, and their one nod at conventionality.

By the time I became a teenager I knew I had to leave, but I had no idea what that would really mean. It was at dawn on a day in mid-July, that I put a few things into an old backpack and headed for the first leg of my journey. I had decided on Boston because it was a fairly easy hitch from Westchester County, NY. I had no real idea of how to get there, but I did have a map, and after the first few rides the people who picked me up helped me navigate. By around 1 pm I was standing in the bright sunlight of the Boston Commons. I had maybe five dollars to my name. But the times were different back then, and I soon found a place to crash and a pathway to survival. I had just turned 14 a week earlier. But I lied to the man who took me in and said I was 17.

This venture into subsistence living lasted about two weeks. Eventually I ended up at a failed music festival in Connecticut called Powder Ridge. Something had gone very wrong and none of the bands showed up, but about 50,000 people did, and a lot of drugs, some of them not particularly pure. There I met a man in his 30s who befriended me. He gave me a ride, which I thought would be to another music festival, but instead he took me home to Westchester.

I never did live "at home" again, though the cycle of dependence and the breaking of that cycle lasted another four decades. The truth was that I had been essentially tossed out by my affluent family. They abandoned me, and I in turn abandoned myself.

My Own Worst Enemy

I also sabotaged myself, and not just once. In fact, beyond just not being a friend to myself, I was clearly my own worst enemy. It was not that I never indulged myself. Self-indulgence was the booby prize; the way bad parents sometimes give in to a screaming kid instead of helping the child deal with her own emotions. In that vein I would over-spend on things I did not even want, drink when I was frustrated, and get into relationships with bad boys just because I liked the way they carried themselves.

What I would not do is slow down and take the steps to build something substantial. I would not bring out my own best. It was clear from the beginning that I had certain gifts. By the time I was 10 I hated the very word "potential." Before my parents let me roll out on my own at 14, they had treated me a bit like a trained monkey. So to sabotage myself was to sabotage them.

I understood all of this by the time I turned 20, but understanding is not the same as being able to heal, or even deal. That took another forty years, though there were some decent years, even good ones, in the interim.

In the early 1970s I headed out west, mostly to get away from my family. I may not have been living with them, but they still loomed large in my consciousness. And, somehow, I was always the loser. It would have worked too, but right at that moment my mother decided to run away from home and the spot she picked was Berkeley, a few short blocks from where I had landed. And soon enough the rest of them showed up. First my sisters, one by one. And, finally my die-hard New Yorker father. The circus had followed me.

An uneasy truce followed. By 1978 the entire clan had repaired to Sonoma County.

I got into real estate and got married. Got out of real estate, got divorced. Bought a house and lost the house to my family, who would let one of my sisters move in. There were three houses like this in 15 years. I always had some business I was trying to start. Anything that would give me sovereignty over my own life. Each of these enterprises was spectacularly under-capitalized. The ones that worked relied on nothing but my cunning and sometimes my physical strength and endurance. House cleaning, catering, and organizing.

During this time, I married three times and divorced twice. Each time my spouse was a man I loved in a way but was not "in love" with. I was essentially settling. I thought if I created stability and did what was expected I would become someone else. It never worked. I never had children with any of them and was in fact unable to conceive. Looking back, that was likely for the best. I would have failed my children. Not in the way I was failed, but it would have happened, nonetheless.

After my mother died, the dynamics completely changed. The sister who was the most difficult for me dragged my now blind father down to Texas, 1500 miles away. I stopped talking to all of them. I was the only one left in California.

I was married to a workaholic. Well, a recovering alcoholic, who had turned to work as an alternative addiction. I went back to school and had a BA in Liberal Studies in 3 years. I graduated with the second highest honors. Magna Cum Laude. No one from my side of the family attended the graduation. BUT—I had achieved a long-time dream. I now knew what winning felt like.

But I still did not know how to be nice to myself, much less be a true friend.

The Winds of Change

By 2007 my husband, Tom, was dying. He rediscovered vodka and it was killing him. For reasons which we agreed upon but no one else understood, I moved out and let his affluent parents take care of him. They blamed me for the whole thing, including his life-long addictions. He died on August 4, 2008. By then I was living with my last bad boyfriend.

I had known Robert since the mid-eighties. I was married when we met at a big Chamber of Commerce mixer. He had a steady girl. There was a spark, but nothing ever came of it. We lost track of each other a number of years before, but there he was, on Match.com which I was perusing just before leaving my last marriage. I wrote, and he answered.

He was expert at pushing every trigger that caused me to abandon myself. I knew it after about two years, but it would take a dozen more years to finally break free. Living with him was as exact a replica of my childhood as I could find. The lack of support, the slightly veiled contempt, the lies and betrayal. It was all there. Punctuated by love bombing and regularly pulling me back in.

After eight years of this he had a big health scare. Heart. I took care of him. This is when he decided to sell the house, which was all his. He wanted to travel. When I asked if this travel would be solo, he told me to take care of myself—without him.

So, I moved to Taos and bought a little house and a business. And one would think that would have been the end of it—but in fact it took another six years. He was a regular visitor and we spoke on video chat almost every day, where he continued to tear me down and side with others against me.

Somehow in the vast quiet that is the mesa, something happened. I was running a difficult business, on my own. I owned my own house. And I was alone most of the time. It was finally quiet enough for me to hear the voices of others in my head and separate them from my own.

And I did not like what I was hearing. Robert and all those who came before me were merely out picturing the way I was treating myself. They disrespected me, but I disrespected myself first. They abandoned me, but I abandoned myself first. They betrayed me, but I betrayed myself first.

It is not easy to raise a child who is a friend to themselves. I was a victim of childhood narcissistic abuse, but it does not have to be so dramatic. And for daughters, it is most important for their mothers to model this sort of self-friendship. Especially not allowing others to mistreat or disrespect them as a mother or a woman or a human being.

When I finally understood the entire pattern, I went back and took a look at what I knew about friendship.

What I found:

At some point in my varied career I studied Alchemical Hypnotherapy, and one of the most interesting techniques in that modality is the study of subpersonalities and the use of a method called conference room. The idea is that we are all one person, but we have distinct archetypical parts within us that heavily influence our behavior and experience of life.

The Saboteur

An example most would recognize is the inner child and the higher self. These internal parts are exactly that—part of us, as distinguished from outer voices, even ones we have internalized. Many are common to us all, such as the judge, the rebel, the lover, and the outer "together" adult whom we almost always choose to present to the world. Other parts are present in some people but not all, and, of these the most dreaded is the saboteur.

In this kind of healing, you can kill off your abusers and rescue the child, but you can't just kill off the saboteur. It is PART of you. All you can do is transform it. And if it frightens you so much that you can't face it, you can never befriend yourself. You must deal with your inner saboteur first before you can do the rest of these steps. If you have the courage for this, the rest is easy.

What Self-Friendship Looks Like

In friendship there is mutual trust. To be your own friend you must trust yourself and your own inner guidance. This means getting quiet enough to hear it and not second guessing yourself constantly. Others who know you well may be able to give advice, but only you know the whole story. It also means being TRUSTWORTHY. You must keep your word to yourself. If you promised yourself you would walk every day for health and then don't, you lose your own confidence.

Respect, care, and consideration. We want the best for our friends. We listen to them when they are speaking and speak kindly to them in return. We think the best of them and give the benefit of the doubt if we think they messed up. These were all places where I failed myself. I stayed with those who had no respect. Robert never gave me the benefit of the doubt and neither did my family of origin. But I always gave anyone and everyone that benefit. I would always choose them over me. When that changed and I became the center of my own life it was like breaking out of prison. I am my own advocate and choose me.

Then there are the things we don't do to a friend and I now won't do to myself.

I don't steer myself wrong. Or lie to myself, or cheat myself. And I don't let others do so either. I protect myself and my own interests. This can come up in different ways. Letting clients and customers pay less than the going rate or fail to pay at all. Going above and beyond for others when they would not do the same. People pleasing. Turning into a pretzel accommodating someone else's needs at my expense. Having people keep me waiting when they shouldn't or standing me up. Now I have a two-strike policy and that is it. And a pre-pay policy so I don't get cheated.

We don't put our friends down or chip away at their self- esteem, and I don't do these things to myself anymore. My self-talk used to be WORSE than what the abuser du jour was throwing at me and that is saying a lot. There comes a time in the life of an abused child when the abuser doesn't even have to work at it, the victim's internalized wicked voice will do it all. I passed that point by the time I was two and never slowed down enough to question it till I was sixty-two.

And by that time, I had broken my own trust over and over again, so it was hard to see that the self-abuse was not justified.

We don't gossip about our friends or speak ill of them behind their backs. But I was all too quick to tell tales on myself. It was a defense mechanism that never worked, but it was deeply ingrained. One of the ways that my sisters joined in the scapegoating was to interrogate me instead of having a conversation and I was so terrified of them that I would explain everything I did as a protective move. Now I have learned to not volunteer things not pertinent to the situation or person at hand. I don't convict myself before charges are brought. And I expect the boundary to be honored.

We don't sabotage our friends or abandon them in their time of need or betray them. In alchemical hypnotherapy the saboteur is one of the most powerful sub personalities and one of the hardest to deal with. Because he or she is part of us, we can't just kill it off. We have to make a deal with it. Because I had betrayed myself so many times by taking less, allowing other people to harm me, and not living up to my own standards, that saboteur was a tough customer. In the end I put him in charge of quality control. Whenever I let my guard down too soon or fall down on self-care, he pokes me to attention.

The difference between my inner life now and five years ago is dramatic. Now the voices inside my head sound like this: "What would you like to do today?" or "Let's make something good to eat, even though it is just us." Or "If you are tired you should rest." Or, sometimes, "come on, you know you have to get that project done or you won't be happy. We can get ice cream afterwards." But most importantly, I say things to myself about how others treat me. If someone is disrespectful or mean or oversteps, I call it out right away. And if it is hopeless, I cut off that other party rather than abandoning myself.

I trust myself because I have become trustworthy.

If this is like you, please take the time to think about how you treat yourself. Are you as kind to yourself as you would be to a friend, or even a stranger? If not, what could you do to figure out your weak points and do better? And if you have a friend who is a people pleaser, and you suspect they treat themselves with less kindness than they do the world, could you find a way to have a conversation about it? Friends don't let friends sabotage themselves, at least not once they have the awareness of what is at stake.

Chapter Three

"In the fury of women comes the power to change the world"

~ *Rebecca Traister, author Good and Mad:*
The Revolutionary Power of Women's Anger

WOMEN'S RAGE

For years I knew the fire of anger as it surged from my depths to engulf all thoughts, along with its more severe partner, rage. There was more than one occasion of wondering if I had been born angry. Looking at my eight-month-old passport photo, I think, maybe so. Dripping with angry sweat-soaked hair that had sprung into sticky curls, my face twisted into a flushed scream while sitting on my mother's lap because I refused to cooperate unless held.

It was decades, several therapists, and a great deal of personal work later, before I learned of the long-term studies on cross-generational prenatal memory cognition and natal trauma.

"Early prenatal experiences, including early trauma, are encoded in the implicit memory of the fetus, located in the subcortical and deep limbic regions of the maturing brain."

".....this can include cross-generational trauma passed from mother to fetus during pregnancy."

~ *The Guest House Ocala*

My introduction to anger didn't stop at birth. As I shared earlier, I was born to, and more significantly, carried by a young woman who had spent her early years in WWII bomb shelters. She lost both parents to that war, and like so many of her age, later married the American Dream. The horrifying reality seemed to defile the fantasy as, 6 years later with me in tow, she landed in Montgomery AL during the struggle for racial equality during the early 1960's.

Her sense of having survived one war, just to find herself transported into another didn't stretch the imagination.

Yet that was just my beginning of knowing the never-safe or settled roiling anger and rageful expression that would define my youthful home. The particulars of the many this's and that's feel unnecessary. I summarize my parents' home as a shroud of alcoholism, untreated mental health issues, the emotions accompanying the decline from affluence to poverty, and a mother committed to raising American children with proper British manners. Just in case that wasn't enough anger-based programming to suit me, by my teens I was forced to accept what I'd long known and consistently buried. I preferred holding hands with my girlfriends to having boyfriends. It was the '70's and I was living in one of the most repressive states in the nation with the broadest number of anti-homosexuality laws. I don't say this to diminish the trials of lesbian and gay people in other areas of the country. It was a dark time for those, of what was then known only as the LGB community. The level of physical, emotional, psychic and legalized abuse I witnessed being leveled upon the members of that community, on a weekly basis, amplified and awakened two goals. Healing my anger and rage became number one. The close second that permeated every cell of my being was a commitment to advocacy for all marginalized humans.

The Repressed Warrior

Even from my early youth something deep inside constantly whispered of my being a natural warrior. During the years of my battle for survival on many fronts this aspect of myself became twisted into the negative side of that warrior spirit. The sad irony was that I had been so angry, for so long, about so many things, and for so many reasons, that while I did find it miserable, I lacked all ability to imagine how to address life differently. The anger and rage had come to feel like an integral component of who I was, both my inner abuser and my single greatest protector. There is no doubt that it was damaging me and my life, but the means of transforming that raging energy into an asset felt illusive. Until...I happened upon some studies that compared the positive and negative traits of female archetypes. While only the first steps of a long journey to refocus my internal energy, it was a welcome entrée to that path. Having something as simple as a designated understanding of the positive aspects to the emotions in which I'd long felt trapped came as a sweet promise of emancipation.

Without going into a deep review, I'll share the top twelve comparative traits of the female warrior archetype. Each is worth evaluating against our own habitual expressions. Their contrast produces the sensation of being trapped in a revolving door and will ring as all-too-familiar for some. Powerful surges of strength that are devolved and weakened by anger, rage and self-depreciation.

See Table 4: Comparative Traits on page 36

Decades of self-reflection, psychological study, brain science research, spiritual journeys, and a virtual obsession with personal development helped snuff the fire's most explosive eruptions. In its wake, what remained felt like a gaping hole that reached all the way into my center. More years followed, with a ferocious commitment to meet myself head-on. Studying the archetypal traits shifted my thinking about anger. I ceased to see it as something to be thoroughly extinguished. By shifting from the idea of positive and negative traits to powerful and dis-empowered traits, great volumes of the belief in my fundamental wrongness started dissipating.

Table 4: Comparative Traits

Positive / Strength	Negative / Fragility
Courage	Hostile Aggression
Resilient	Procrastination
Bravery	Hostility
Playful	Critical
Positivity	Potentially Cruel
Empathy	Judgmental
Persistent	Inflexible
Loyal	Vindictive
Self-Reliant	Aloof
Confident	Co-Dependent
Creative	Vain
Disciplined	Lacking Focus

Women's Anger

You would be hard-pressed to find a woman who does not understand many of the insidious ways females are taught, from girlhood, to fear and feel shame for their anger. It's a power more significant than what society has given females the right to wield. The combination of fear and anger is an internally toxic cocktail that easily spills out to harm those in proximity.

Everything that can create, can destroy, and vice versa. The juxtaposing effects of nuclear energy, if used for war, or when applied in medicine, is an example with which we are all familiar. Just as we learned arithmetic and conversational skills, anger requires understanding the principles of constructive execution to become a valuable tool. Being repeatedly admonished with false teachings such as, be nice, lower your voice, and anger is not ladylike, have repressed generations of females. When was the last time you asked a young girl what she wanted to be when she grew up and heard the reply, "polite"? Having permission to our own anger revoked from our earliest days has robbed women of understanding how to use it as a tool of creation. At this point we can be easily run over by our anger's negative surge.

In her book, Good and Mad: The Revolutionary Power of Women's Anger, Rebecca Traister states:

> *"In the United States, we have never been taught how noncompliant, insistent, furious women have shaped our history and our present, our activism and our art. We should be."*

Being angry is not a conviction of being bad or wrong. It is an indication that you are conscious enough to realize something external doesn't line up. Anger can be a red flag alerting you that the circumstances you are witnessing or experiencing are off, threatening or counterproductive. This is a call to pay closer attention and not suppress the feeling that is bringing you an important message.

Bestselling author Glennon Doyle describes in her book the productive use of anger this way:

> *"Anger is a gift that's pointing us in the direction of the change that we need to be a part of making. The key is not allowing it to make (her) like the people (she's) fighting."*

The Cost Women Pay for Internalizing Rage

Countless women chronically suppress their anger. The strength of their childhood and our society's programming has them twisting themselves into pretzels. They are emotionally crippled by the fear that if they feel the anger, they might be compelled to acknowledge that they are outright mad. Having had the right to be angry withheld since youth, females grow up without being shown productive approaches to address the situations that evoke those feelings.

Over the years I've heard more women than I can count, speak of how they never get angry. I've met them as clients, in professional settings, and social environments, in large numbers at spiritual community gatherings, and more. They speak of their lack of anger while it presents itself in clearly recognizable ways. Everything in their lives is held in a chokehold of control. Something as simple as a five-minute conversation to ask a single question must be scheduled weeks in advance. Nothing in their lives that produces sound is ever allowed to rise over three on the volume dial, particularly their words. Should someone utter a swear word in their presence, they are appalled. Sometimes they will even request the person not use such *negative* language around them. They have sacrificed their voice, their instrument of communicating with the world. The language they choose is tempered to present the picture of unflappable tranquility. The fear of their own anger peeking out through an undetected crack in the façade has reduced them to virtually obsessive self-monitoring. Some may succeed in continuing this pattern for decades. Nothing is ever allowed to ruffle the atmosphere. A greater number find their anger revealing itself in the most unpleasant, sometimes heartbreaking ways. Whether it is a shocking outburst in a public setting, an unexpected rant triggered by a specific conversational topic, or the kids finally confessing the effects it had on their childhoods. Anger, like water, always finds an egress. People pleasing is one of the more insidious ways women keep their anger well contained. If I can make everyone happy, they'll all see I'm a good person and everything will be okay. But it's not. It's one more exercise in self-denial. A passive-aggressive expression of self-abuse via repressive behavior.

Witnessing the way some members of the generations junior to myself are progressively speaking out, I had dabbled in the hope that the tide was changing. Then I came across a body of studies indicating otherwise. One from the series was written by psychologist Sandra Thomas, PhD, chair of the PhD program in nursing at the University of Tennessee, where she has been studying women and anger for 15 years.

"Although younger women may believe they're comfortable being assertive, when it comes to anger, they still struggle. A college woman, for example, may be freer with profanity, but she is still reluctant to tell her boyfriend she's angry if she thinks an outburst will drive him away".

A list of the most common symptoms of women's suppressed anger, as revealed during large-scale studies by a string of top university medical centers include:

Chronic headaches, digestive issues, insomnia, anxiety, depression, heart attack, obesity, and substance abuse. Stuffing one's anger may cause those at your dinner parties to rave that you are the most graceful hostess they know. However, if concretized into a life pattern it may also become deadly. Quite simply, internalized anger doesn't disappear or dissolve. It continues to rage in ever stronger ways, but held within, your mind, organs and emotions become the prime targets. As long as we are breathing there is never a time when we cannot turn the effects of buried anger around, by acknowledging and redirecting.

Owning the Power of Anger

Channeled constructively, anger becomes a vehicle for being heard, empowered and bringing about radical evolution. This has always been and will always remain true. Suffrage, Civil Rights, the Equal Rights Amendment, LGBTQIA advocacy organizations, #MeToo, Black Lives Matter, #NeverAgain, the Parkland School shooting survivors March for Our Lives. Then there are the many unknown heroes who wade into the thick of cultural injustices, small or vast. They will courageously grasp the hand of another human who has been knocked down. Each of these represent a positive application of that otherwise debilitating energy called anger.

Anger is a fight, flight or freeze response. When triggered it provokes the limbic system to produce adrenaline, cortisol and some 1800 stress hormones. This is what churns through the veins of a mother, a tiny little woman, giving her the strength to lift the back end of a car that has her child pinned. We've all seen that story. When pointed in a constructive direction it can propel us out of bed to give, whatever our 'it' is, one more try. This time with conviction! Anger can propel us into the liberating position of leaving that unhealthy workplace culture and taking a wholehearted chance on our own dream.

That doesn't mean we will never again feel as if we are lying under it instead of directing it. It only means we've become more committed to our strength than our fragility. As Les Brown is famous for saying,

> *"When life knocks you down, try to land on your back. Because if you can look up, you can get up. Let your reason get you back up."*

It was my own experience, and what I've had the privilege of witnessing through others that helped me grok the core of Les's message. When our reason for learning to direct our anger outdistances any excuse for not doing so, that 'why' will always propel us forward.

Do I still feel the hot rush of anger that clouds my thoughts and rages static through my senses? Only, during the majority of weeks. Racial injustice. Religious persecution. Domestic violence. Human trafficking. Gender inequality. Violence against the LGBTQIA community. I could go on, but the point is that on most of those days I'm learning more about how to direct my anger, instead of being its prey. When I do let that slip away and find myself in the pit, I remind myself of 'why' it's essential to live my whole self. It's quite simply not in me to rest as long as I can offer grace to any other human in a world in which people are treated inhumanely for doing nothing more than being who they inherently are. The broken side of anger will never let me live freely or empower anyone else.

Modern-day Mighty Woman: Sandra Bargman

Sandra Bargman is a lifelong creative, intuitive, and curiositive. She inspires and teaches through entertainment, counseling, and coaching.

Anger and the Reluctant Leader

I was recently talking with a friend who asked me about taking over the leadership of a group to which we both belonged. I told him that he should take over the role. We both laughed a lot during this conversation, and I accused him of being a fellow reluctant leader. The moment that phrase rolled off my lips, "the reluctant leader", I was enamored. I loved it and so did he, googling it immediately only to discover it was already a "thing", but I wasn't too upset knowing I couldn't lay claim to coining the phrase. I was strangely encouraged that it was already out there, and I wasn't alone.

The most unforeseen choice in life can put you on a path full of unforeseen awakening and fulfillment. In the early 90's I made the strange and jaw dropping decision to move away from a bustling life as an actor and performer in a bustling metropolitan area to a life in a very remote one. This big city girl, with matching big city hair and shoes, and nary a piece of flannel owned, moved from NYC to a 3000-acre nature preserve and biological research station in a small Brigadoon of a town in upstate New York. In a nutshell, I was terribly angry at Life and needed some quietude, which I got in spades with my shocking move, landing in a small cabin in the woods, smaller than my NYC apartment, resplendent with a wood stove and a composting toilet, dubbed unsurprisingly "The Throne."

I'd say it was my love for my then boyfriend that fueled my monumental leap, but I'd be lying.

Our little cabin on the preserve was nestled by a huge pond, with a path around it that I would walk, sometimes with my love and more often alone. The woods and this experience intrigued me, as I walked through three distinctly different habitats. One, a young forest, small trees with lush undergrowth, swaths of sunlight filtering through. The second, more mature, a bit darker. Finally, a hemlock forest, majestic, formidable, and magical--it always seemed as if a wood nymph or nature fairy should be peeking up from one of the gnarled roots.

One night I had a dream about the hemlock forest. In this dream, it was nighttime, with a bright full moon as I started down the path. When at last I got to the hemlocks, moonlight was dappling down through the branches and everything was alive with an expectant quality.

In the embrace of the hemlock forest, I began a ritual.

I searched for a spot in which to lie between some jutting roots, and when I found it, I lay back, resting my head in a base crook of a tree. Immediately, my body began to tingle from head to toe. My breathing became rhythmic, and an inner pulsing began in my heart region. Slowly it grew more persistent, filling my entire body. Anticipatedly, I started to split open. With no surprise on my behalf, my body simply opened up in a long line from my chin to my pelvis. As I opened, a bright white light came shining out, straight up into the trees—and from within, another me sat up as if sleeping and was only now awakened. This new me was iridescent, sparkling with light. She looked around and finally stood up, stepped out onto the forest floor, turned to look down at the old me still cradled in the hemlock roots. Knowingly, the old me smiled up at the new me and slowly began to close herself back up, as the new me bent down and picked her up, hugging the old me to herself, and began to walk, slowly in the moonlight through hemlock to the edge of the pond. As this new me walked, the old me that she was carrying began to crumble and dissolve to dust, floating out across the sparkling, moonlit water.

It was with Mother Nature, that I began to howl with some real power and for the first time in my life, I could begin to face my anger and my rebellion. Clearly my subconscious, with this epic, mystical event, was ready to look at my anger and transform, but was I? Acknowledgment was the beginning. I had much more of this work to do, but this was the first step: Why was I so angry, about what, and with whom?

Why Are Women in This World Angry?

Any woman on the planet can agree that there is a tidal wave of women's rage. I have only to mention sex trafficking, genital mutilation and the #MeToo movement to conjure collective deep rage. On a less dramatic and more universal level, gender inequality in society and in the workplace are core places to experience our anger. Studies suggest there are some common routes to anger for women, most notably our feelings of our powerlessness and injustice. Women are paid less, they are not as valued in the workplace, and when they hit glass ceilings it's very hard for them to earn more.

This imbalance continues into the domestic arena. When a woman is working and she comes home from work, she feels she must do so much more than the man does. When it comes to child-rearing women are far more responsible than men. A lot of women do not feel listened to, they don't feel valued, they don't feel appreciated, and they don't feel supported.

Young girls and women learn early, most notably from their mothers that there are penalties for displaying anger. Why do we learn as girls to ignore those feelings?

I came into this world with the belief, the knowing, that I was here on Earth to contribute to Life. My mother told me that when I was around the age of three, I walked into the kitchen with my hands on my hips and announced to her that I was here on a MISSION. I knew I had something to say. I am sure you knew you did, as well.

But also, I was to learn the well-known and demoralizing story of "Too Much". Too loud. Too bossy. Too self-confident. Too sensitive. Too needy. Too pushy. Too crazy. For the record, I have been called all of these. I AM all of these, according to those in my circles for whom my exuberance for life and my engagement in society has triggered. And, in response, I have twisted myself into multiple incarnations to fit in and be accepted, so much so that I have lost my voice, lost my self-respect, and felt myself the victim, not only by those I perceive have kept me down, but by myself.

I was raised by parents who came of age in the 50s, when girls were sugar and spice and everything nice. My parents were the quintessential good parents, the good daughter married the good son, prone to following the rules, side stepping confrontation and fitting into suburbia. My mother was my best friend and greatest fan, and I lived her unrequited dream of performing. My father, angry at his own parents, tossed aside his natural rebel spirit for parenthood and took his anger out on my burgeoning creative thinking and preternatural ability to communicate. It was all there in my DNA. The good girl and the angry rebel.

My Anger

In her powerhouse book, Rage Becomes Her, Soroya Chemaly said *"There is not a woman alive who does not understand that women's anger is openly reviled."* By the time she was a young adult, Chemaly had developed the firm belief that she was not someone who experienced anger. She didn't identify feelings of anger in herself at all.

How many of us can relate to that? As the perpetual optimist, one who walked through the world with a large, enthusiastic life force as a child and a young adult, I certainly can.

When I was 9 years old my parents moved us to their hometown of Pittsburgh, and I started in my new elementary school two days after we arrived.

My first day began well. I enjoyed the curiosity of the other school children toward me.

After lunch, we had a half hour of playtime outside. There was a large parking lot abutting a large baseball field. This particular day, there was a game of keep away going on, with two teams. I meandered across the concrete to the field, longing to join the game. Would I be asked? You see, the game was being played by boys only. Turns out, they were as curious about me, as I was eager to play, and finally I was put onto one of the teams. It didn't take long for them to see that I was a good runner, so of course, the ball was given to me. And I was off. No one could catch me. Turns out,

44

my running caught the attention of the girls back on the concrete, and some of them came over to watch, along with some of the boys, huffing and puffing. The game came to a stop, and I could feel the admiration of the boys, some looking down, and dirt kicking. And then the bell rang, the spell was broken, and we were back in class.

The next day couldn't come fast enough. Eager to play again, when I got outside to the pavement, I heard my name being called. "SANDY!" It was coming from the other side of the pavement. Then I saw a line of girls, all holding hands, walking across the pavement and I could hear them all shouting my name! My heart skipped a beat with surprised happiness. As I ran to get closer, my heart sank. "We hate Sandy. We hate Sandy." The entire line of girls, in unison, chanted over and over.

It wasn't the boys, with whom I had played. No, I had their admiration, however begrudgingly. It was the girls who organized, eager for a take down, competitive and cruel.

Lesson learned. Being my full self, my proud, athletic, playful and powerful Self did not bring support, acceptance and celebration, but rather jealousy, alienation and non-communication. I share this early event that had such a breathtaking effect on me, simply because it illustrates what we as women face over and over again from other women throughout our lives and careers, from those whom we would wish the most support.

Not getting what we want and getting what we don't want. This is the source of the ANGER. As an actor, a counselor, a public speaker and coach, I believe we all want greater connection and therefore better, deeper communication. How do we get real, get brave, get risky, and communicate effectively around our anger? The first step is getting in touch with it.

Young women are socialized firmly with the idea that anger is incompatible with femininity and with understanding oneself as a good person.

Case in point.

My professional life began with highly competitive conservatory training at Carnegie-Mellon University, followed by a career devoted to acting, singing, and performance based in New York City. I became aware of my anger when I was in conservatory. A rabid anti-smoker at that point in my short life, I became a smoker, a powerful self-harming "smoke screen". I'll never forget in one of my earliest acting classes, I was doing a 2-person scene with a fellow student in which I needed to become enraged. My partner and I rehearsed relentlessly and finally we were ready to present our scene to the class. We emoted, rolled on the floor, threw props, finished, and took our places for notes from our instructor as well as our fellow classmates. Over and over, from each classmate and from my instructor, my note was that they didn't believe me, that I wasn't angry enough. I was speechless and confounded. I was so unaware, so detached from anger, and what it even meant for myself, that I couldn't conjure it. By the time I was a young adult, I had developed the firm belief that I was not someone who experienced anger. Like Ms. Chemaly, I couldn't identify feelings of anger in myself at all.

I'm Not Angry; I'm Passionate, Assertive

Little girls learn early, Ms. Chemaly said "that there are penalties for displaying anger, we know that there are risks to expressing your needs. Which is what I think anger is – it's a self-defensive emotion. It's provoked by care or threat or indignation. The question is, why do we learn as girls, which we do, to ignore those feelings? What possible good can come of that, to us?"

At their core, both fear and anger are rooted in feelings of control. In most cases, when we experience fear, we may feel as though we have lost control of a particular situation, circumstance, or individuals. Anger is the unaware attempt to gain control, to combat feelings of victimhood and helplessness. Anger...

46

- thwarts love and happiness
- destroys relationships
- crushes the spirit of children
- isolates us from everyone around us

A spectrum of poor mental and physical health outcomes can be traced back to mismanaged anger. There are higher incidences of depression, binge drinking and smoking among women as evidence of the damage internalized anger is wreaking. Depression - and there are many types of depression - is anger turned inwards. Many women never learn how to express anger, which in turn makes them angrier.

So How Does My Anger Relate to My LEADERSHIP

It's been said that anger is the mask of pain and grief. I had the stereotypical life of an artist – many thrills, accolades, successes and magical adventures alongside many heartbreaks and misfires, jobs taken away, jobs given away. My sadness and pain cut deep. In addition to being a terrific smoke screen for my feelings of vulnerability, anger opened the door to my righteousness, power, and moral superiority. Hadn't I been wronged by those less talented, those looking to hurt me, those with jealousy, those chanting "we hate Sandy"? My self-righteous anger was addictive, and I was free to be bitter, critical, and judgmental.

The heartbreaks and losses are to be expected, but often, they felt planned, vindictive. Hadn't I whittled myself down enough to make everyone comfortable? I rest assured that my subsequent anger was repellent to the very people I wished to attract.

But here's the deal with this kind of anger...I can't predict anyone's behavior but my own.

Yes, righteous anger is real and necessary. Yes, victimization occurs. I am in no way looking to diminish the outrage and anger caused by severe trauma and victimization. I am, however, suggesting that we must search for reconciliation. If I, if we, cannot find a way out of feeling helpless, then we cannot find our voice. We cannot change our worlds.

At some point I must decide that I am not helpless. That, ultimately, I am not a victim, and that I do have choices.

I Finally Listened to the Call of Leadership

In my 40's, I was called to step out of the proverbial closet, and to serve and lead in a spiritual capacity. I enrolled in seminary and after finishing the 2-year program, was ordained at St John the Divine as an Interfaith/Interspiritual Minister. I went onto another two years of seminary obtaining an advanced certification in spiritual counseling.

I quickly learned that the spiritual world was no different from the world of show business. Understanding spiritual principles and living them were, I was to learn, two vastly different paths. The spiritual world enraged me more than the world of show. A quick story to illuminate this point was a dinner I had with a Seminary Mentor. I had completed my second seminary training and had invited my mentor to dinner to celebrate. After a lovely meal filled with lively conversation, I leaned in to make a particularly exciting point, very animatedly gleeful, after which I was promptly told by my mentor that I could never counsel or minister to people with that level of energy and intensity. In essence as I heard it, I could not be myself. Not surprisingly, I chose to feel hurt and angered by this exchange, rather than to simply see it for what it was. Just his opinion.

As truth would have it, I am a natural born leader and I've always known it. I understand I walk in the world with natural authority and most of the people in my inner circle would claim that I am fearless. But I also have a distaste for top-down hierarchy, knowing that I am also a natural born rebel. In addition, I have always felt like I existed in the liminal places. The edges. I was easily bored in the world of show business and impatient with and turned off by the preciousness of the spiritual community. The cruel competition of the former, and the lack of engagement in the latter played heavy on my heart, more often than any joy experienced. I was looking for realness and aliveness. In childhood, I wanted to change the world. As an adult, I fought to not be changed by the world, so I chose to stay at the periphery of each tribe, never fully committing to any one group. This afforded me easy movement, liminality, or so I thought. What it really offered me was the classic recipe for self-righteous anger. In her book, *The Leadership Gap: What Gets Between You and Your Greatness*, Lolly Daskal discusses leadership archetypes, the strengths, and weaknesses of each. I quickly identified mine: The Rebel Leader is driven by confidence, and the dark side of the rebel is the Imposter, plagued by self-doubt. The Hero Leader embodies courage, and the dark side of the hero is the Bystander, who is fearful.

In 2014, I started my own business, Sacred Stages, LLC that combines my performance background with my ministry. The idea of Sacred Stages was born in seminary, out of my own longing. While I enjoyed studying the world's religions, I was not a part of any one of them. As we've established, I'm not a joiner. So...where do I go to have an expansive experience with community? To the theatre, of course, where the stage is my altar.

That year I wrote, produced and performed my first one woman show under the umbrella of Sacred Stages, *"The Edge of Everyday"*, which was constructed like a ritual, blurring the lines of cabaret, ritual, and performance art. It was my own personal ritual of blurring the lines of my old understanding of performance, that of playing a role, with finding and speaking my own voice in performance. The cabaret rooms of Manhattan became my "churches", and my caba-ritual, my "preaching". In the show, I explored through song and musings, the blurred edges between the light and darkness, the complexities, and dichotomies of life. It mirrored my internal experience and edges and spoke to the growing anger and political polarization on the American and global landscape.

The show received rave reviews, had sold out performances, held great promise, but I also knew that it would receive push back. My vision was to create a new genre, and lead with my own voice, so when the inevitable push back arrived, the sadness and anger resurfaced. I had a choice to make. Was I going to get to the bottom of this or keep recreating it? Was I going to finally embrace my anger as an agent for change, rather than a roadblock to leadership, to sharing my own voice? In his book, "Leadership Pain", Sam Chand writes,

> *"Reluctance to face pain is your greatest limitation. There is no growth without change, no change without loss, and no loss without pain."*

Answering a calling is no small and easy feat, it is fraught with challenges. And realizing a vision does not happen without struggle, strife and loss. When you hold a powerful point of view, there will always be those who disagree and strongly. I needed to summon my deepest sense of self trust and courage. As author and inspirational speaker Simon Sinek has said, "If everyone agrees with you, it probably means that you don't stand for anything."

I made a paradisiacal discovery; one I could never have seen coming. I was afraid. I was afraid to lead with my own voice and message. My anger reflected my fear. Anger may be the mask of pain and grief, but more importantly, it is the mask of FEAR. Like most women, I had learned at a tender age that it was more important to be liked than it was to be respected. I had learned early on to people please as a strategy to feel safe and in control. I wanted to please, I wanted to be loved and revered. I did not want to experience push back. No, I did not want to see the faces of others twisted with misunderstanding, ridicule, cruelty, dislike or jealousy, true or imagined.

Anger is BOLDNESS in action if we are willing to look within and to get real about not only its source but also to transmute and focus it. Otherwise, the rage fire will burn you and your dreams down. Owning the fear and anger is the passage out. And it is the key to unlocking the door of judgment and impatience and moving into vulnerability and authentic communication. I genuinely believe women want greater and deeper connection, which leads to authentic, effective communication, and a sharing of one's true voice. THIS IS LEADERSHIP.

The "WHY" Game

When you find yourself in a situation, or experience when you are reacting with anger or any other emotionally triggered way, stop, get quiet and ask yourself why.

- Why am I angry (or fill in the emotion)?
- Why does this make me feel angry?
- Why do I feel so triggered?

Stay quiet and present to the answer that comes to you. Don't judge it. Just stay with it. When you're ready, treat your answer with the same questions. With each answer, try to simply stay present to the answer without judgment...and keep backing out and asking why.

More times than not, you will discover the underlying issue, and potentially your own participation, and will be able to cool the fire and make new choices that feel more empowering. Remember, we can use anger for many reasons, and my personal favorite is self-protection.

Let the World Touch You

As you walk through your day, allow yourself to simply notice the gifts that are presented around you and take a moment to acknowledge them with gratitude. In each moment there are many opportunities to see the world anew. The kindness of the cashier. The dog who barks at you with its tail wagging. Children laughing. Flowers blooming. I can highlight here by mentioning a focus on noticing Nature. Nature is ever miraculous and ever devoid of anger as I learned during my stint living in the woods upstate. Taking the moment to stop and acknowledge these gifts will flood your mind and body with dopamine, the "feel happy" chemical, and you begin to retrain your mind to connect to beauty rather than defaulting to anger. Trust me, 15 minutes a day will make an enormous difference.

Chapter Four

"Other women are not my competition. I stand with them, not against them."

~ Anonymous

BUILDING A LIFE

I think of my adult life as having started when ultimately, out of necessity I left the east coast for the heartland in pursuit of a career I had not yet identified. Without missing a beat, I found myself in the middle of the corporate world of the mid through late eighties. At that time notably few women held roles of true professional authority. Numerous had a position and occasionally even a title and maybe a bit higher income. However, being awarded the authority equal to one's title was a rare and elusive unicorn.

Being one of those anomalies provided me an up close and personal view of the lengths to which women of that age were willing, eager even, to stretch in order to undermine a female peer. I've long referred to this as my period of sailing through fences, having received a swift kick in that direction from another female. The memos I never saw that were said to have been hand delivered or placed on my desk. Bear in mind this was long before the trackability of email or text threads for disputing such claims. The condescending looks and remarks intended to set me off-balance, moments before an important presentation. There was an overriding attitude of superiority and ostracization.

I understand how, on the surface, these may seem like small things. Possibly the missed messages were unintentional oversights or the person delivering the diminishing words was not herself that day and no harm was intended. Maybe I wasn't being intentionally excluded. There simply wasn't a connection. That tradition of gaslighting produced the very excuses used every day to insure it was the one being targeted who remained off balance.

Ultimately exhausted, frustrated, convinced of my ineptness and feeling unable to take one more step, I resigned. The first morning I awoke after fulfilling my announced period of departure I was shocked to find myself unable to rise from the bed. Physically and emotionally spent, there was simply no energy. Actually, I was beyond spent. It felt as if I was clinging to the edge of a cliff with nothing but my index fingers. A full year passed before I was close to fully functional.

Fast forward 30+ years to 2022 and the stark reality is that it remains all too common for women to find themselves in this exact situation. Untold numbers of smart, industrious, capable women have put all they had into a position they initially imagined as the ideal fit for their skills and individual passion. Only after years of struggling to balance the love for their role with the impossibility of the workplace culture do these women walk away. This is frequently less a voluntary choice than a physical, emotional imperative. They are so far over their own edge that reestablishing both physical and emotional balance requires an extended period of time for a complete recharge.

Comprehending the scope, nuances and intricacies of what women have endured to lift us up to where we currently find ourselves is mind-spinning. Yet mental, emotional, intellectual and psychic violence is still experienced by women in the workplace on a daily basis.

Contributing Factors

In any discussion about woman-to-woman incivility and competition, the obvious question that arises is, 'why'? Numerous factors and motivations come into play. Through my many years of mentoring women, a single theme has consistently presented itself as a key to understanding.

It is most candidly stated by, Susan Shapiro, in her bestselling book, *Tripping the Prom Queen:*

"There's something irresistible about tripping the prom queen. No matter how good our own lives are, no matter how much we know better, no matter how we try to remember the importance of female solidarity, every single one of us has at least one moment of looking at a powerful female rival and savoring the fantasy of bringing her down."

While this can sound simplistically vicious, it's actually a physiological, medical phenomena. The German word, schadenfreude shaa·duhn·froy·duh, a compound of *schaden*, "damage, harm" and *freude*, "joy", describes the spiteful, malicious pleasure experienced in witnessing the misfortune of others. This used to be dismissed as simply the dark side of human nature. In truth it's so much more nuanced than that. Brain-scan studies have shown schadenfreude as correlating with envy. When we witness another's fall from grace, it can induce a chemical release within the dorsal striatum of the brain, literally causing us to feel pleasure.

A striking example of schadenfreude that has become viral is our societal addiction to negative press. The tabloids rake in hundreds of millions of dollars on a weekly basis, fifty-two weeks of every year. Consider the exultant ripples of joyful gratification that rip across all social media platforms when a celebrity or political figure trips. Our twenty-four-hour news cycles more closely resemble a contest for who can present the grizzliest of human behaviors. No small amount of this has carried over into what is called mainstream media. Far more than an equal share is directed at women, particularly those who have achieved great heights, in any arena of life.

One example of this trend was an article published by Forbes on some of the challenges Sheryl Sandberg has faced. A comparison was presented between the way the media has treated Sandberg, versus how male executives have been treated when they drop the ball. One reporter referred to Sandberg as tainted, as if she were a quart of milk left in the refrigerator for too long. There have been calls *by* feminists *for* feminists to *publicly* condemn her. One leading US newspaper published a big, bold headline reading,

"Sandberg Can't Have it All." Who of us has ever read a headline declaring that a male CEO, of a top company, can't have it all? Painfully, a majority of the diminishing expose's about women in power, from Sandberg to Angela Markel are written by women.

Examining the core of competition, research confirms it to be an ancient component of human nature. Whether we are intentionally pushing to win a race or unconsciously trying to suppress another, we are responding to one of the oldest parts of our biology, the quest for survival against both real and imagined threats.

Substantial evidence points to our patriarchal society as a lead instigator in driving the competitiveness expressed amongst women. Another protagonist is our culture's capitalistic drive. We each experience a constant bombardment of our 'less-than' factor from advertisers telling us what we must look like or wear. The wealth-envy created through messaging of what we should own has a crippling effect on human psyches, particularly women, toward whom the majority is directed. The resulting wounds to our self-image result in a projected flow of hostility toward anyone who might appear to possess all we lack. This can extend to leverage, seniority, or the potential to bypass us in ascending the professional ladder.

A recent study published in Harvard Business Review presented that:

1. The average woman is less competitive than the average man.

2. Women shy away from competition because they're less likely to think they'll win.

Both of these points identify ways that female childhood programming impacts women throughout their careers. Self-confidence is essential for setting down the fear of being targeted by workplace incivility and going all out in pursuit of our professional aspirations. Developing effective skills toward this end provides an indispensable sense of personal security.

Below are a few of the most dynamically effective tools I have helped women cultivate.

Identify Allies

There are always going to be women who appear smarter, more successful, more creative and more confident than ourselves. Let's not lose sight of the fact that this is only a small part of their story. We cannot know what's behind their veils. Comparing ourselves to anyone else is a form of internal competition that traps us in a state of mental and emotional self-devaluation.

When encountering a woman who can claim greater accomplishment than you currently possess, seize it as a teaching moment. Respectfully and confidently share your appreciation for what she's achieved. Ask if she'd mind sharing one of her favorite strategies with you. This can range from her key to success or self-confidence, to how she cultivated audacious courage.

Everyone enjoys being appreciated. Whether this ends up being a one-time conversation or evolves into an ongoing source of support is fundamentally irrelevant. In either case you have established yourself as an active learner. Further, you will be remembered as someone who is dedicated to expanding her knowledge base and interpersonal skills. If the woman you approach doesn't choose to share, you still benefit. She's just given you insight as to how she addresses other women in the professional environment. Move on. There will be another, more gracious associate around the corner. *Knowledge breeds fearlessness.*

Give Yourself Room to Make Mistakes

When any of us reflect on our greatest breakthrough moments, they virtually always follow periods of having either found ourselves wading knee-deep in quicksand or flat on our backs. It is a common habit of our neurology, specific to the limbic system, that when we do find ourselves in the swamp or turning ourselves into pretzels, our minds leap directly to what I call the, 'what if's' trap. What if I get fired and can't get a new job? What if my partner asks for a divorce and I end up losing everything? What if I blow this presentation...and on it rolls. We drive ourselves deeper and deeper into self-recrimination for being so unforgivably human.

Rather than dwelling on worst-case scenarios, try an alternate starting point by refocusing in a productive direction. Take a few moments to reflect on all the value that past mistakes have provided. How much did you learn from, what seemed at the time, a life-upending mis-step?

As successful entrepreneur Catherine Cook states:

> *"If You're Not Making Mistakes, then You're Not Making Decisions."*

Giving ourselves permission to make mistakes helps us still the critical mind. When we silence our own negative self-talk, we have far more energy to apply sound critical thought into any decision before us.

Perfection is Overrated

While perfectionism is practiced by both sexes women are far more likely to hold it in reverence. For many this started as long ago as being, "daddy's perfect little girl". As of the end of the third quarter of 2020, American's had spent $71B on weight loss. $47B of that, right at two-thirds, was spent by women. This same year women spent an average of $813 a month on skincare and makeup products. Let's note that this was during a devastating global pandemic when we were locked down and engaging in minimal personal interaction. This is a glaring lens into how profoundly our nation suffers an obsession with perfectionism. The harshest reality being that women are the most victimized by these unrealistic standards. They also lead the charge, directly to the diet products and cosmetic counters.

As long as we seek that ever-unattainable state called perfection, in any area of life, we will never find ourselves to be enough. Not worthy-enough. Not smart-enough. Not clever-enough. Not lovable-enough. Not entertaining-enough. Not thin enough. Not attractive-enough. And this is fertile ground for the fear that drives competition.

It's time to create a new pinnacle. I like awesome because its point of reference is completely relative. We each have different standards for what is awesome. Now is the moment to give ourselves ample room to take a radical stance. Practice focusing more attention on the moments when you are pleased with who you are as a person. Celebrate your successes as a parent, partner, employee, and contributing member of our global community. Treat yourself regularly for being a person you actively appreciate, respect and honor. Being simply and magnificently awesome provides space for gentle and continuous growth. Additionally, seeing the awesomeness within ourselves presents a tempting invitation to explore our individual uniqueness while celebrating the same in those around us. Most significantly, research by top university medical centers has revealed that people who develop the habit of engaging in positive self-talk demonstrate stronger problem-solving skills and express greater creativity. Further, they exhibit more effective coping mechanisms resulting in reduced periods of stress and anxiety.

Modern-day Mighty Woman: Janine Hamner-Holman

Janine Hamner Holman is a sought-after keynote speaker in the areas of Leadership and DE&I. She is the CEO of J&J Consulting Group and Founder of DEIBPA (Diversity, Equity, Inclusion, & Belonging, Professional Association).

The Cost of Incivility

In 2008, in the midst of the economic downturn, I decided to undertake a major career shift. After spending almost 20 years in non-profit senior-management and fundraising, I got a job in public affairs for a Fortune 200 company. Pretty quickly, I realized I was very good at it and – over the next 8 years – grew my book of business from $2.5 million to over $33 million in annual revenues.

I was sure that this was the last job I would have. I'd give them 20 or so years of service and retire from there. As one of the youngest baby boomers, I still had it in my head that people were supposed to work someplace for a long time...and that a job equaled security. And, for the first time in almost 20 years, I was working for a big company. If I did good work, which I was doing because I really liked my job, they would be loyal to me and I to them.

Looking back now, it would seem sweet – albeit naïve – if it didn't have such a ghastly ending (spoiler alert!). Also, as one of the last of the baby boomers and a child to parents of the Silent Generation, I was taught to be happy to have a paycheck and do whatever it took to keep it.

The trouble was, I was also the proverbial frog in the pot of water when it came to the organizational culture in which I was swimming.

Let's call my boss Ouida. Ouida came from a difficult family and was herself a functioning (more or less) alcoholic. She was like the girl in Longfellow's poem: "And when she was good, she was very, very good. But when she was bad, she was horrid." Ouida managed a team of a dozen managers, both directly and indirectly. She always had a favorite - and always made it clear who that was. When you were her favorite, she shone a spotlight on you and sung your praises to the rest of the team and people who were accountable to you. "Janine's so great. Look at what she did. You should all be like Janine." It was lovely in the sun. The problem was, there was always someone else in the doghouse. Worse than the doghouse. Under the outhouse. With the shit.

"Steve is such an idiot. Steve, are you really that stupid?!? Look, he can't do anything right. Look at what Steve did." This too was public. Ouida seemed to enjoy undermining people's credibility when you were under the outhouse – in front of colleagues, customers, partners, anyone and everyone.

You could see it coming. The problem with being in the sun was that you knew the shit was coming. And it was going to be a HARD fall from grace.

But I thought I could handle that...because "I'm good at this job, I'm a strong woman," and I knew that I was totally competent, and a job means security, right?

So, I hired a coach and went on antidepressants.

The 8+ years that I was with the company took a huge toll on me. In 2016, I went back to the psychiatrist (for the second time) to discuss how I could better manage myself and my mental health. I was demoralized, depressed and felt lethargic. Much to my surprise, my doctor put me on immediate medical leave. I was out for 6 months – working to combat the depression, exhaustion, and overwhelming lack of confidence and a lost sense of self that had taken control.

After 6 months, I was cleared to return to work. But, if I tell the truth, it really took me an additional 6 months to get back to myself. I spent an entire year rebuilding my feelings of self-worth, confidence in myself, my abilities, and the belief that I had something to contribute.

The impact of Incivility

Why am I telling you this story? Because it's way too common in organizations today, and it has a particular cost for women. In her seminal work, *Mindset: The New Psychology of Success*, author and researcher Dr. Carol S. Dweck writes

> *"Many females have a problem not only with stereotypes, but [also] with other people's opinions of them in general. They trust them too much...Girls learn to trust [other] people's estimates of them...Boys are constantly being scolded and punished. When we observed in grade school classrooms, we saw the boys got eight times more criticism than girls for their conduct. Boys are also constantly calling each other slobs and morons. The evaluations lose a lot of their power."*

What Dr. Dweck is pointing to is the drastically different way in which cisgender boys and girls are socialized, both by their caregivers and by each other.

Girls are praised for being cute, sweet, polite, pretty, and nice. Through this, they learn to praise and evaluate each other for these same (and similar) qualities. Boys are physically and verbally aggressive with each other, joke about farts and other bodily functions, while calling each other names. As a result, and as a group in which there are lots of exceptions, women tend to be impacted more severely and deeply by harsh criticism than men. Let me be clear, men are affected too. Toxic work environments are horrible for all people regardless of gender. What I am emphasizing here is that women are significantly more likely to internalize the criticism and experience it as doing harm. It's like the difference between doing a bad thing and being bad. Many women, including me, have construed other people's criticism such that it has the potential to affect us as though we are bad, instead of a more dispassionately observed conclusion such as "I did something that this one person thinks wasn't great."

I recorded an interview today for my podcast, *The Cost of Not Paying Attention*, with Dr. Bruce Harman, a passionate and energetic executive coach focused on helping his clients achieve extreme levels of trust in their leadership teams. He's a 3-time TEDx speaker and leadership professor from Los Angeles who married his first childhood love. After surviving a rare bone disease and enduring 4 spine surgeries, he ditched his corporate job so he could help leaders bring more love and trust into the workplace. Pretty cool, right?

Bruce and I were talking about how common it is for people to be disengaged at work – 85% of employees are just 'phoning it in.' The biggest reason: incivility, microaggressions, toxic workplaces, dysfunctional organizational cultures, or a culture like I was in – with a manager who had no training (true of 90% of all managers!), who thought that micromanaging and being cruel were effective strategies for success and was rewarded with a promotion for what she was able to compel from her team.

One of the most shocking dynamics happening in organizations is the frequency that incivility is demonstrated in our workplaces. According to Gallup, the percentage of workers experiencing incivility has risen from 25% in 1998 to 99% today. 99%!! What makes it even worse is the way that our brains are wired to manage hostility.

When we see someone being mistreated, talked down to, getting eye-rolls, being ignored, being left out of important conversation or 'forgotten' to be included in a meeting...and all the other ways people get treated uncivilly, our brain processes this as a threat in our environment.

Our Brain's Response

More than a decade ago, I became interested in neuroscience and how our brains work – both in our self-interest and many ways that don't actually help. This is one of those times! It would be really nice if our brains would realize, *"That's happening to them. Over there. While it may make me mad or sad, it's not happening to me. I'm safe."*

Nope.

That's not how our brains work. The abuse might as well be happening to us. Our brains release a cascade of hormones that sends our system into hyper-alert. Our heart beats faster, our breath quickens, and our lungs open wide to take in the most oxygen possible...and send the extra oxygen to our brains to increase our alertness. Our senses become sharper and nutrients flood our bloodstream. Our muscles tense. We're getting ready. It's fight, flight or freeze time. And all of this happens before the visual centers in our brain can process what we're seeing. It's all automatic and incredibly fast.

And it doesn't matter if we're under attack or it's the person in the cubicle next door. Our brain's sensitivity to danger is like that of a squirrel that's gotten into a cup of espresso!

This makes it even more critical that we bring civility into the workplace. It almost seems like an antiquated word. Civility. It means being polite, respectful, kind, courteous.

I want to create a distinction here between being nice and being kind. According to Websters, nice is being *"polite; pleasant; agreeable; or satisfactory."* Ultimately, it's about not rocking the boat. Kind is defined as *"of a sympathetic or helpful nature; gentle; affectionate."*

We can be kind and "speak truth to power." We can be kind and candid.

When I am kind, I honestly and genuinely care about the people with whom I am talking. I want what's best for myself and for them. I care about how they are doing. And I am willing to tell the truth – because I care about them.

One of the things that I have learned is that I can't be honest like this while I'm also being "nice!" Speaking honestly with care to others can DEFINITELY rock the boat. And nice is all about making sure the boat never rocks. Often, however, what we need is to have our boat rocked! It's how we learn, change, grow, expand, develop. I can rock your boat kindly, with care. I can't rock it and be nice. How can I tell you you're doing something that's hurting others, causing them to be less than they are...or hurting yourself and causing yourself to be less than you can be...and cause you no distress. It's impossible. Unless you're a sociopath – in which case you'll care not one lick anyway – you will have a reaction to realizing that you're doing something (or not doing something) that's inhibiting yourself or your people. I think it's actually a prerequisite for transformation.

Feeling uncomfortable is necessary before we make a different choice. And the only thing most people hate more than the way things are is change! So, most of us need to get uncomfortable before we are willing to go through the pain of doing things differently.

This is 100% the opposite of how most people are conditioned! Many people are conditioned by society, parents, school, work, friends, partners, life to be nice and NOT candid with people. The truth can rock the boat and we (particularly women) are not supposed to do that.

Other people are conditioned that it's a "dog-eat-dog" world. In this paradigm, we are taught that we must oppress, intimidate, covertly manipulate, and create power over others to get what we want/need.

People Pleasing

Along the way, many people, mostly but not exclusively women, are conditioned to please others at all costs. This is what's often known as "people pleasing." I, like some of you, am a recovering people pleaser.

People-pleasers are some of the "nicest" and most helpful people you can meet. We people-pleasers spend much of our time helping others. We're great organizers. You can always count on us for favors. We always make time for our family and friends. We're generous to a fault and incredibly loyal.

However, it comes at an incredible cost. Us "pleasers" don't have the word, "no" in our vocabulary. We burn ourselves out, being what others need us to be, and can lose sight of our own goals, needs, and dreams. We forget to "put on our masks first before helping others!"

For many of us "pleasers," all of this comes from a very human need for safety. Every human is driven by this need. There are entire sections of our brain that are solely devoted to ensuring we are safe. But for those of us who are habitual people pleasers, something got crossed up along the way.

We "pleasers" take it too far. For many of us, the need for safety has been translated into people liking us. More problematic still is how our very identity can become based on the approval of others. Most people have some kind of fear of rejection and/or fear of failure. My personal flavor was fear of being "in trouble."

This fear led me to turning myself into a pretzel in order to stay out of "trouble" since the ultimate impact of this "trouble," in my mind, was a loss of respect, love, affection, and connection with whomever I was seeking to please. My mind's commitment to this belief drove me to being overcommitted, resentful, exhausted, over-stressed and ultimately, physically ill.

It's an important pattern to break. It's a journey and I invite you to join me in it, if you see this pattern as one you have been acting out.

Another place where women are in more jeopardy than men is that we are literally hard-wired to be concerned about 'the wellbeing of the herd.' We have an inherited 'scan vision,' which is critical for paying attention to the health and wellbeing of everyone…often to the exclusion of ourselves. It's also why we can know where our husband's keys are, where the ketchup is, and where the dog's ball is hiding. This explains why many women have a challenge with telling whether there's enough room to pass that car on the freeway traveling at 80 mph or track a hockey puck on the ice.

Men are hard-wired with 'track vision' that enables these skills. Their brains are wired to track fast movement, which was immensely helpful on the Serengeti and has been hard-wired into our genetic makeup.

These fundamental differences in wiring, however, also make women much more susceptible to being 'people pleasers' and to being physically harmed by toxic cultures.

A Duty to Do Better

Even more challenging, many of the perpetrators of office toxicity are women! While some of this connects to lessons that women learned in the workplace combined with the quest to succeed in male-dominated organizations, women often engage in, frequently unconsciously, competition. For there to be competition there are two key conditions that must be met: scarcity or the perception of scarcity, and sameness. You must have both.

If there's just scarcity – well then there's just not enough. For competition, there must be sameness too – you could pick A or B. Me or You. If you and I are too different, there's not enough sameness and we won't compete.

But, if there's enough sameness and a perception of scarcity, our brain reads it as "GAME ON! Time to compete!"

Some days and in some situations, we decide, "Nope, I'm taking my marbles and heading home. I'm not competing today." This is usually when you have more, perceived, power or status than me.

While we can't do anything about our biology, our brain's <u>first</u> instinct – to always leap to "GAME ON!" – we can do a lot about what action we take next.

When there's scarcity and sameness *and power* all in the mix, this is where I believe we have a duty to do better. When you and I are in a situation where I have some kind of power over you (I'm your boss, your more senior colleague, your mentor, your mother, your older sister, your spouse/partner etc.), I have a responsibility to pay attention to my response to my brain's signal of "GAME ON!"

There are all kinds of other reasons women may engage in unhealthy competition. We may have internalized an idea of what women are supposed to be and are trying to hold ourselves and others to that patriarchal standard. We may have externalized our feelings of self-worth and are trying to compete for resources with which to validate ourselves. Some of it is definitely determined by socialization – our families, society, and cultures, not to mention race and socioeconomics.

One of the many great things about our brains, however, is our neuroplasticity – essentially a fancy way of saying that our brains can change! So, while I can't do anything about my first "GAME ON!" response, I can do everything about my second one.

I am my thoughts, behaviors, programming and beliefs...until I bring self-awareness or someone else helps me see it.

With awareness, I can go from being my biological reactions, to choosing my actual responses. Once I see my behaviors, I bring awareness. Now I can see my programming and choose the reality into which I want to live.

For women, who one of my mentors calls *"the Velcro of the Universe,"* it's especially important. When we bring awareness, we can choose to break down and remove the barriers so we can dwell together in love and connection. And, in case that sounds too "kumbaya" for you, we want to dwell in love and connection so that we can increase the potency of our will to create the lives and world we want to experience.

Practices like mindfulness and meditation can come in very handy when we're looking to retrain the neural pathways and programming in our brains. Breath is a big part of all these techniques and it's a great place to return over and over again when we find ourselves hooked by status or competition or wanting to take someone else down or out.

Take a deep breath.

It literally calms down the chatter in our heads and allows us to be present. It enables us to reset our brain out of our limbic system and back into our prefrontal cortex where we can think and make conscious decisions.

Keeping eye contact – not in a crazy stalker kind of way but in an "I'm here with you" way also helps us to stay present and calm our fight or flight (or compete!) instincts.

What is Possible

We all know that trust is the foundation of every healthy relationship – both with others and with ourselves. When we show up first for ourselves and then for each other, we begin to develop trust.

When I tell you the truth, we develop trust. When I mean what I say, say what I mean, and follow through, we deepen trust. Trust is critical to taming unhealthy competition. To paraphrase Dr. Brené Brown, the thing that I most need to be connected to you is vulnerability. And it's the thing I am most afraid to show you in me.

When we bring awareness, add mindfulness, cultivate trust, and add in vulnerability we have an opportunity to really be a stand for ourselves and each other.

We can be kind. And civil. Respectful.

Our lack of civility is taking a huge toll on human health. It's not just me who went on antidepressants. Depending on the organization reporting, 10-17% of the population is on antidepressants. The number is even higher among women. After two years of COVID-19, it's higher still.

Incivility is having a profound impact on the quality of work, people's experience of work, our economy and our pocketbooks.

Writer Annie Dillard famously said, *"How we spend our days is, of course, how we spend our lives."* For many of us, a large portion of our days are spent working. It's safe to say our jobs make a huge impact on the quality of our lives.

According to a *Harvard Business School* survey, 94% of service professionals put in 50+ hours a week. But we're also massively disengaged – remember 85% of all workers are 'phoning it in.' An easy way to begin to get people more engaged is by creating more connections at work.

Humans are herd animals. We need connections to survive and thrive. With an increasing amount of our time spent working, creating meaningful connections at work is a great way to begin.

What if we were all more civil? What might be possible? For ourselves, our gender, our families, our institutions, our nation?

Chapter Five

"The way you achieve your own success is to be willing to help somebody else get there first"

~ *Iyanla Vanzant, Author*

ON THE SHOULDERS OF MIGHTY WOMEN

Years of conversations about the what's, how's and why's of mentorship have taught me that mentors differ as vastly as those receiving the support. Who can serve as a valuable advisor at any given time, relies wholly on where we are in our lives. What we are ready to learn will inform their approach to being a successful guide. Ever a fan of origin stories as a passport to greater understanding led me to pursue the etymology of the word.

The genesis I found most fascinating comes from Executive Coach, Patricia Fripp.

> *"According to Greek legend, the goddess Athene liked to come down to earth disguised as a man named "Mentor" so she could advise the young son of Ulysses. (The Greek root "men" means remembering, thinking or counseling; we still use it in words like "mental.")"*

In keeping with the current day definition, variance is the key. Occasionally we are blessed by mentors whose guidance leads us forward for an entire lifetime. These are often seniors who bestow a legacy of wisdom. Many of these advisors are discovered during our younger years. On more occasions than I can recount the wisdom bequeathed by my dear paternal grandmother has served me in very good stead.

Mentors who walk beside us for extended periods, encouraging our pursuit of a particular goal are far more prevalent. Period specific mentors can be our greatest champions. Expressing belief in our ability to bring long-held visions to fruition invigorates our self-confidence. Partnering with the right mentor when starting a new

71

business or pushing for a big promotion can help us sidestep potential pitfalls. Being tutored in the most effective ways to identify our best next steps helps reassure us that we have the tools to make sound choices. Simultaneously, it sharpens our critical thinking processes for big decisions that will arise in the future. Potentially, the greatest benefit mentoring offers is the encouragement to get back up after we fall. Even during the most discouraging periods, the benefit of having someone consistently assure us that 'we can', cannot be overstated.

In recent years mentorship has become an industry unto itself. Yet, the truest definition of the word does not limit it to the rigid structures of current-day application. Many times, our most valuable mentor can be unofficial. Someone who graces our lives for just one season. Despite deviating from today's perception of a mentor, they uplift and enlighten in ways that sustain us. These effects can sometimes continue for the duration of our lives. Foregoing the formalities of structured mentorship, their gift is often received by witnessing the way they walk through their own days.

From semi-formal to completely non-traditional expressions, my earlier life was blessed by the mentorship of 4 amazing, powerful, and generous women. Ranging from 31 to 43 years my senior, their life experience and wisdom blew the top off of every limited perception I'd formed about our world, and more impactfully, regarding myself. The cumulative effect they had on one wide-eyed and hungry thirty-something young woman is something for which I remain ever-grateful. Each of the women to whom I am about to introduce you, while now long passed from this world, lifted me onto their mighty shoulders leaving imprints on my heart and a consciousness that continues to grow unto this day.

First Came Sarah

The first of these beneficent way-showers entered my life at a holiday gala. Immediately enamored of her sharp wit and graceful spirit, I spent much of the evening ingratiating myself into group conversations that included her among their numbers.

My reflective discomfort at having fallen into adoring puppy mode quickly faded, when a couple of days later Sarah rang and invited me to lunch. Only two meetings later she asked if I'd ever considered a life mentor. While at that point I'd not heard the term, the timing could not have been more ideal. I was at the end of my rope with the corporate world and too exhausted, on every level, to strategize where I would go next.

As the first year of our association whisked by, I walked away from every conversation treasuring some golden nugget. Each proved relative to directing me toward the full and rich life I had long craved. One time it was just a word validating my inner sense that the time of changing careers was quickly approaching. Some of you may be personally acquainted with the deeply unsettled gut-knowledge that it's time to go. Possibly you've experienced how it can run hand-in-hand with a complete absence of clarity as to how or where. A single word of belief in your ability to land on your feet can taste like a great wave of fresh oxygen. Sarah's understanding of this showed up as thoughtful gems dropped into unrelated conversations.

On several occasions Sarah invited me to join her and several female peers for dinner or tea. Among these worldly, socially, culturally and politically savvy women, it was clear to me that I possessed nothing of value to contribute. Sitting through that first dinner attentively spell bound, I made every effort to silently become one with the shape of my chair. Well, of course that was never going to fly. This produced my next level education in communication; learn how to formulate a solid question. One that is sufficiently open-ended as to require the questionee to respond, expansively. That would not only rescue me from the hot seat but provide a myriad of fascinating new knowledge.

The topic of my family never entered the conversations between Sarah and me. Yet, I always assumed that her skillful insight to people had informed her that my parents were dispossessed of any communication skills, whatsoever. She repeatedly drew me into situations that required further development of my personal communication skills in order to be an active participant. Through this, Sarah gave me a passport to the world.

Learning Women's History from Makers

About eighteen months into my relationship with Sarah she received an invitation to attend a think tank in Dallas. It was the late '80's, and the event was a gathering for feminists & lesbians. The focus was to strategize means of forwarding gender equality. When she firmly stated that she wanted me to go in her stead I was convinced she had lost her mind. In response to each of my progressively more flimsy protests, she simply smiled and talked about how exciting it was that I would be attending such an important and rare event. I barely slept for the three days prior to catching my plane and hid in my room for the first half of day one.

Finally, gathering my courage, I ventured into the afternoon session. In attendance was a woman we'll call Maeve, who had been deeply involved in both arenas since the early '60's. Several times over the course of the event I found myself invited into group conversations where she was either a participant or the leader. Numbers were exchanged, followed by months of long-distance conversations. Our relationship was based on complimentary sensibilities. I was driven by a desire to learn and she was eager to educate. As our connection evolved, so did my respect for her expansive knowledge of women's history. I was fascinated by the ways it weighed against the intricacies of the current-day issues.

Maeve became my go-to for anything relating to female empowerment and awareness of our collective history. She was always forthright when offering personal insights, which helped me establish a comfort within the relationship. Many times, she initiated introductions to other women she thought I should know. All these women had traveled the long road to individual upliftment. The most intriguing conversations Maeve and I had were rooted in her wealth of *first-hand* historical knowledge. Being a mentor in the truest sense, I was regularly directed to some body of research material, and given the space to discover my own answers and form individual perspectives.

What I valued about Maeve above all her many attributes was her commitment to give each of those around her space to disagree. This lasted as long as they could quantify their reasoning. Otherwise bored of the conversation, she would wander off. She taught me, and many others the importance, of not just listening, but hearing the unspoken motivations that drove people's beliefs. Over time, I came to understand the value of hearing over merely listening to such a degree that I began incorporating it into my own teaching.

My Dear Fannie

DivInc, Championing diversity in the tech startup ecosystem:

> *"Mentors come in all shapes, sizes and pedigrees. We've been exposed to them throughout our lives in some capacity or another. The teachers that inspired you in school, that rare breed of friends who have a knack for succeeding in everything they do, the family members who collect and share a lifetime of lessons."*

Such was the case with my dear Miss Fannie. Intuition is the only possible explanation for why I experienced the privilege of meeting her, as I'm not in the habit of abducting people standing at bus stops. Leaving a grocery store one dark, cold morning, the rain poured so heavily I could barely see through the windshield. Nevertheless, I happened to spot the tiny bit of a woman bundled in a big coat that was covered by a rain slicker. Her little grocery trolley was covered with another plastic cover as she stood waiting at the bus stop. Without a thought I spun my car in that direction. Having barely shifted into park, I called for her to "Jump in before you drown!" Her attempt to decline, "Oh no honey. I'll be fine," came too late. With my hands already on her soaked grocery bags and trolley, I carefully tossed the whole lot into the back seat. Acquiescing via a big smile, she slid into the passenger side.

Inching through the wall of rain Miss Fannie pointed the directions toward her home while regaling me with hilarious stories of her life. I heard about the two times, thirty years apart, that her late husband had tried to teach her to drive. Each to no avail. Since his death 5 years earlier, she had depended on the bus or an occasional cab.

Possessed of *old school* manners, Fannie wasn't going to stand for my immediately dashing off after having helped her. By the time we'd consumed our cans of cola with her special homemade fried onion and ham sandwiches on bread she'd made early that morning, we each had a new friend. This being late fall with nothing but rain followed by months of snow heading our way, at Fannie's acceptance, I appointed myself her official driver.

Each Saturday, I would pick her up promptly at 8:00am. Groceries, the pharmacy, flower shop, and anywhere else Fannie wanted to go, we went. Laughing our way through every morning, we always returned to savor whatever special lunch she had planned for us. Food she'd learned to make from her earliest days back in Little Rock, AR, and that I'd never had the pleasure of tasting but fell in love with, at each new bite.

It was a Friday morning when Fannie called to say she was taking an unexpected trip and needed to pick up some necessities. Throughout our time together, she had shared many stories from her life, starting from when she was born in AR in 1929. They carried through to how her husband had moved her to Tulsa and the many years since. However, it was one event above all others that introduced me to the heart and soul of who Fannie was.

Beyond having mentioned once or twice her years as a teacher, she had never previously expanded on the topic of her career, until that morning. Dashing about town to collect her supplies, Fannie talked about her days working with what we now refer to as neurodiverse children. She spoke of how inadequate the expectation to teach them from the same curriculum as the greater student body made her feel. Fannie's down-home good-sense, combined with sharp intellect told her this would never help these kids sustain themselves through life.

Following her heart, Fannie designed a completely new program. It utilized items from daily life, newspapers, grocery lists and calculating (pretend) money. Fannie wanted a platform that more closely fit her student's long-term potential. Her program was declined by both local and state education boards. Long story short, some years later Fannie happened upon an article detailing the work Eunice Schriever was doing in education. Pen to paper, she immediately sent a letter, including an outline of her curriculum. Mrs. Schriever contacted Fannie and the program had found its champion.

Driving Fannie on her errands, listening to this story, I was struck by the never-before-known audacity of this tiny, unassuming woman, equaled only by her dedication to her students. Our day together and her story concluded with the news that Mrs. Schriever had personally invited her to a gathering of leading educators in Washington DC. Fannie was to join the number of, now retired, professionals who had made valuable contributions to kids' education.

Asking for help in preparing for her trip had proven a most revelatory day into my friend's tenacity and grit. I'd known and treasured Fannie's natural humility since having met. The clear strength to never give up on something important fueled by 'old-school' ingenuity revealed new dimensions of my friend. What I learned from Miss Fannie remains a gift of inspiration and mentorship for which my heart still pays tribute.

Last and Oh-So-Far from Least

Not the least of my wonderful influencers was a 5' tall powerhouse of a woman from California's Bay Area. I was blessed with Merlin's presence in my life after a call from her daughter, saying that her mother was flying in for a visit. Thinking of ways to entertain her, the idea had struck that 'mom' and I would hit it off famously. Would I be open to a lunch date?

Merlin epitomized the definition of mentorship offered by Caela Farren, Ph.D.:

> *"It [Mentorship] is a learning and development partnership between someone with vast experience and someone who wants to learn."*

She had spent her professional life building and organizing political races. Her greatest pride was having been instrumental in securing the California presidential nomination for Bill Clinton, not once but twice.

Referencing back to an earlier mentor, one of my paternal grandmother's many gifts was a legacy of political fascination. Her longtime friend, then Congressman, Carl Albert, was frequently among her dinner guests. Long nights of rousing conversation, often filled with vigorous debate, were the faire of the day. This well established interest in all things political fueled my excitement for meeting Merlin. She was a woman well familiar with the machinations of the political world. When she dropped from the sky into my life, I was already primed and every inquisitive cell in my body jumped into high alert. What will it take for women to gain greater political, professional and societal status? Personal freedom? How can we address the more treacherous political hurdles with greater effectiveness? What are the trigger points that we, as women trip on, inadvertently setting ourselves back? The more I wanted to understand, the more she reveled in sharing insights from her vast wealth of hard-fought knowledge.

While we did have many phone conversations I only got to spend real time with Merlin on two occasions when she visited her daughter. My season with her was fleeting but full. What she poured into me during our short friendship established a solid foundation on which to continue building. Having a guide to where women stood within the greater political spectrum was one part disheartening, one part liberating. Even more illuminating was the education she provided around the covertly established hurdles that limited women. Those we would ultimately have to leap to finally claim equality for ourselves, and an equitable future for all females.

The Gifts of Mentorship

As these four fascinating women revealed themselves to me, through equal measures of humility, brilliance, and audacity, I learned the power of mentorship. Their ease-filled presence coupled with the way they interacted in the world was a complete education unto itself. They modeled a vision of potential I had not previously imagined possessing.

Over time these beloved way-showers introduced me to greater numbers of women than I had previously possessed access. I met an ever-expanding body of females of every age, culture, race, history, education and socioeconomic representation. As they freely shared stories of their joys, triumphs and shocking tales, I realized that I was neither special or unique. This may sound self-diminishing but was in fact the polar opposite. It was a sincere relief to no longer feel like an outsider within my own life, to know that I was not alone. I was a woman. Not just a woman, but a true and full woman on a planet among untold numbers of other women. Each of whom told their own version of the disorienting journey of having wrestled with questions and doubts mirroring my own. It was the grace of being generously lifted onto the shoulders of these mighty women, and the many who followed, that shaped me into who I am and continue to become.

We All Need Mentors

The increased pace and complexity of our world is accelerating daily. Events and circumstances we never previously imagined, now require our being poised to pivot on a dime. From parents wading through the foreign language of tech to support their kid's educational journey during a pandemic, to professionals whose sites are set on the C-suite, navigating the landscape is complicated. To their own detriment, great numbers of women are adamantly resistant to some of the most effective support available to each of us. Mentorship. Whether citing it as frivolous, or claiming they know their business well enough to make a mentor redundant, they cheat themselves of one of the more valuable tools in life and business.

From Mary Stutts, author of 'The Missing Mentor',

> "Women are way behind in developing and utilizing mentors. Women need to create a development plan to gain experience, and be deliberate about each step of the way. Even in executive positions, very few women have any sort of development plan and that is scary".

Mentors help us maintain a connection to our own magnetic north. Their stories offer abundant insight to potential pitfalls and inspiration to believe our goals are achievable. Personal development and leadership books are wonderful tools that the many on my own bookshelf will attest to my referencing frequently. Yet, nothing duplicates the power of a personalized, no nonsense conversation. Mentors provide the space to engage in communication so transparent that your hidden hopes and fears become naturally revealed. The honesty and candor with which they pose tough questions can be both inspiring and affirming. A truly great mentor can expose the internal hurdles you've not yet gathered the courage to view honestly.

Mentors are the gift that keeps on giving. Their only agenda is to guide you toward achieving your vision. By listening with full attention, they hear what is carried in your deepest heart, and can envision the clearest path to fulfillment. It is well known that until her passing in 2014, Dr. Maya Angelou was Oprah's most beloved mentor. Why would someone like Oprah Winfrey, with all her many accomplishments, often referred to as *A National Treasure*, have a mentor to whom she regularly turned?

> "A mentor is someone who allows you to see the hope inside yourself."
>
> ~ Oprah Winfrey

Why Too Few Women Mentor Up

A rally cry for women to rise to their greatest potential has been sounded. The dialogue around the need for our unique contributions can be heard from all sexes, cultures, socioeconomic groups, and in every corner of the world. Allowing ourselves the essential guidance for this to occur starts with turning down the volume of our egos. Most of us know those inner voices that tell us we're fine, we have this, we know what we're doing. While all three may be accurate, there is no shame or diminishment in seeking support to up-level our game.

COO of Facebook, founder of Lean.org, former V.P. of Global Online Sales and Operations at Google and regularly named on Top 100 Most Influential People in the World lists, Sheryl Sandberg, offers this assessment on the value of mentorship.

> *"The importance of having a mentor (person who will advise you) as well as a sponsor (person who will use their influence to advocate for you) with regards to career progression cannot be overstated, the wisdom of mentors will help avoid mistakes and clean up ones that you weren't smart enough to avoid."*

Effectively pushing the needle forward means having as much of ourselves as we are capable of expressing, available in our lives, every day. It doesn't matter whether we're considering pay equality, leveragability, equality of borrowing power, or determining what we want to create next. Women need mentors, every bit as much as men. The argument can be made that women getting a late start in this arena, are in greater need of mentors.

The process of opening to guidance requires a willingness to reveal oneself. Exposing dreams and goals to another provides clarified access to uncultivated levels of ourselves. Mentors help us expand our knowledge base, language and awareness of the newest cutting-edge systems. We might only have access to many of these assets through a more broadly connected professional. As with the cases of both Sarah and Maeve, a powerful benefit of mentoring is discovering your circle of influence and additional support expanding via key introductions.

Identifying Your Ideal Mentor

Only you can identify the ideal fit in a mentor. Start by first getting candid with yourself about how far you are willing to stretch on behalf of your own best interests. The questions in the following section will help you determine if you are ready to take the necessary steps for achieving results.

- Are you open to disclosing both your fears and desires?

- Is the journey of self-evaluation and receiving honest, candid feedback one to which you are open?

- Does your goal inspire you enough to take on the hard and sometimes sticky work of development to achieve life changing results?

Having spent some quiet time sincerely reflecting into each of the previous areas, you are ready for the essential next steps. These questions are designed for the period immediately following your initial meeting with a potential mentor. They will help you to clarify the experience. Determining if this person is a good match for both you and your goals is fundamental to pairing with the right person. These questions are also valuable to revisit on a periodic basis. Assessing your progress to insure you remain on track is required to fulfill your goal. Remember; your goal is, ultimately, your responsibility.

- Do I feel mentally, emotionally safe with this person?

- Do I get the sense that this individual will hold my better interests at the forefront of our collaboration?

- Do I feel this person truly hears my stated goals and desires?

Relationship Building with Your Potential Mentor

Prepare for your initial meeting with a potential mentor as you would any important interview. Having your goals clearly outlined in your mind, or better yet on paper, will serve you and the mentor candidate. Preparing advance questions assures you of gathering valuable takeaways during the meeting.

The following are some well tested questions that I've used over the years when considering someone as a mentor. They have also provided a clear launch point for friends, colleagues and even clients.

Why Do You Mentor?

As Simon Sinek famously teaches, "Start with Why." Starting with an understanding of why a person mentors affords sound insight as to whether the two of you might be a good fit.

How Long Have You Been Mentoring?

Longevity of mentoring can indicate how finely tuned the individual is in relating to and guiding a mentee.

What is Your Area of Specialty?

Remember, mentors are not one size fits all. It's important to know if a person receives more enjoyment mentoring in one area over another.

Where Would You Start if You Were Me?

Succinctly outline where you are, where you want to be, and what you see as your primary obstacles. Follow up with the simple question; "where would you start if you were me?" This demonstrates to your potential mentor that you are serious about mentorship. It also reveals that you have clarified goals. From there the ball is in their court to decide if they would like to help bring your vision to fruition. Similarly, their response will offer insight as to whether you connect with their mentoring style.

What is the Most Significant Challenge You've Helped a Client Overcome?

Understanding the level of complexity or challenge the potential mentor is comfortable addressing is helpful in knowing if they are right for you.

What was the Big Mistake You Made That You Now Help Others Sidestep?

Eleanor Roosevelt advised, "Learn from the mistakes of others. You can't live long enough to make them all yourself." Everyone makes mistakes. A mentor who shares from the wisdom gained through their own mistakes is a valuable asset. On the other hand, one who is uncomfortable speaking of their mistakes may turn out to be highly critical of yours.

What Are You Still Struggling to Master?

Any mentor worth working with will be able to acknowledge that learning is a lifelong journey. Being willing to offer a brief insight to one of their own unmastered areas indicates a level of humility. This speaks well to their overall character and ability to give you space for growth.

What is the Primary Thing You Consider Before Mentoring Someone?

Mentoring is not a one-way relationship. It is as important to determine if you are an ideal mentee as it is to know if this mentor is a good fit for you. If they are not enjoying the experience, it will be hard for them to engage fully enough to be a valuable guide on your journey.

What Frustrates You the Most When Working with a Mentee?

Clarifying the mentor's boundaries will inform you on two levels. Do you find them reasonable? Are you comfortable with the stated expectations?

Change Your Life; Mentor Others

Mentoring is one of the most fulfilling roles I've ever undertaken. The excitement of witnessing someone achieve a potential that you had detected but that was previously hidden to them, is beyond measure.

Equally, it is one of the most challenging experiences of my life. There is an ongoing need to develop a new language for expressing the same principle. People have different ways of hearing and learning. In order to serve the goal of understanding all of one's various mentee's, flexibility of delivery is a must. In return, I've experienced the gift of witnessing how vastly expansive that single requirement is to the mentor's own knowledge base.

An article in Harvard Business Review revealed that studies indicate mentoring others is one of our best avenues for honing our leadership and communication skills, as well as establishing us as an organization builder. Little has enhanced my leadership skills as much as both being a mentor and receiving mentoring from others. It reveals the holes or weaknesses in our expertise. Developing comfort with uttering the all-too-often dreaded words, "I don't know," is a powerful demonstration of leadership. Particularly when followed up with, "I'll find out," and doing so to be able to deliver the information at your next meeting. Modeling that it is okay to make mistakes, and that none of us knows everything, about anything, is a useful validation for a mentee and helps keep us humble as mentors.

It was those first gifts of mentorship, received from Sarah, Maeve, Fannie and Merlin that informed me of the power and importance of sharing our wisdom forward. The ability to witness someone emerge into more of who they are is a humbling journey. I find mentoring younger women who are ready to take on the world, but not yet sure of all the steps in the dance particularly satisfying. Seeing who they become, all they accomplish, and the lives they impact, is a continuous reminder of why I mentor. To mentor someone, is to inspire them to pass that support forward. It is from this continuum that we all rise.

Mentoring Toward Success

The most skilled professional mentors I've known and had the privilege of working with spent years to decades developing a broad range of skills before mentoring others. Additionally, they were each wise enough to continue receiving their own mentoring throughout their lives.

Beyond all else, truly gifted mentors don't choose that path, as much as they recognize it in their heart and soul as something they *must* do. From this heart-driven space, a mentor can reach beyond their own specific knowledge. Sharing the deeper and universal wisdoms they learned along the way is a generous gift.

> *"In order to be a mentor, and an effective one, one must care. You must care. You don't have to know how many square miles are in Idaho, you don't need to know what is the chemical makeup...of blood or water. Know what you know and care about the person, care about what you know and care about the person you're sharing with."*
>
> ~ *Dr. Maya Angelou*

One such person is Jane Bradley. She is a celebrated artist, mediator, respected mentor, award winning businesswoman, teacher, and writer. The following is an outline Jane created as a template for women to implement in understanding mentors, the experience of mentoring, and how to create outreach for connecting with your ideal mentor.

"As a long time mentor, please allow me the privilege of sharing some personal thoughts on mentoring. I have been personally mentored by some of the best in the world. My cowboy (rancher) Dad and my cowboy (medical doctor) husband.

I have loved living my life as a serious, successful, and serial entrepreneur. All along the way, there have been mentors – both in my personal life and in my professional life. I was just smart enough to know that I didn't know what I didn't know. I was willing to watch, listen and learn. In turn, I became a mentor and have loved working with mentees. Their success always feels like my own success.

I wish each of you happy mentoring and a life filled with teaching while learning and caring while sharing."

What is a Mentor? Do you need a Mentor? What are the traits of a good Mentor?

The definition of a mentor is: Noun. "an experienced and trusted advisor"

For both the experienced business owner and for those new to business, developing a sustainable relationship with a respected and trusted advisor is one way to jump start your business, grow your business, and avoid all the pitfalls that exist in today's business world.

Traits of a Great Mentor

There are good mentors and not so good mentors. These are the undisputed traits of a great mentor.

Your Mentor Must Be:

1. *A good listener. This is a team effort; your mentor* should not ever fall into an instructor mode.

2. *Knowledgeable.* Your mentor needs NOT be knowledgeable in your exact business endeavor. Rather, they should be knowledgeable in the practices and procedures for success in any business.

3. *Flexible.* An open mind is essential in the mentoring process. All options should always be "on the table" with your mentor.

4. Able to *give constructive feedback* and feedback that you are comfortable in following. Trust is a non-negotiable requirement in mentoring.

5. *Honest, candid and an abundance of curiosity.* These are great traits to find in a mentor.... but then, these are great qualities to find in all associates, co-workers, and friends.

What Can You Expect from Mentoring?

Your mentor should provide:

Advice: Mentors can provide answers to questions and make suggestions that allow you to follow YOUR dreams to success.

Perspective: Because of their experience, your mentor can provide perspectives that you may not have considered.

Enhance Your Skills: In contrast to Business coaches or consultants, mentors are invested in helping mentees develop business skills to serve you for the long haul.

Confidence and Encouragement: Confidence plays a critical role in making business decisions, dealing with associates, gaining new clients, and the world in general. Mentors can instill and ensure confidence in you, the mentee.

Finding That Perfect Mentor

Mentors come in many forms, as do you, the mentee. Mentoring can be likened to a marriage. If it works – it's great. If it doesn't – it's hard to fix. Finding the right fit in a mentor is essential to your success and to the process. Trust your intuition about compatibility. If it doesn't "feel" right – it probably is *not* going to work to your best advantage.

Some tips to help you select a mentor:

- *Know your goals (both short and long term).* What do you want to accomplish and what are the professional qualifications of the proposed mentor in relation to your goals?

- **Who do you look up to?** Who do you admire? Why? Where would you like to be in the next few years? Has this person "been there and done that?

- **Be aware of your existing network and your social media contacts.** The more aware someone already is of you, your values, your dreams, and your abilities, the more effective they will be at mentoring you.

- Look at your **Stakeholders.** This is anyone who has a *professional* interest in your success. Your accountant, your business partners, your landlord, your service providers. It is worthwhile to Google the word "Stakeholders". After you have read and digested this information, determine who is in this group. Then, make a list in connection to you and your business.

I wish each of you happy mentoring and a life filled with teaching while learning and caring while sharing."

~ Jane Bradley

Chapter Six

"If you want to master something, teach it"

~ *Yogi Bhajan*

COACHING

Becoming a professional coach was never something I'd set my sights on, despite years as the go-to within my various circles. When someone needed an attentive ear, a calming presence or helpful feedback, my phone would ring. Coaching began when following a presentation, a woman approached exclaiming, *"My brother really needs you!"* Intrigued by her urgency, I agreed to meet him the following day. Our conversation revealed two things. I truly enjoyed who he was as a person, and his self-perception was plagued with distortions. My second client showed up a few months later, after a speaking event. A couple approached unbidden, to ask if I would meet with one of their mothers.

This pattern of future clients finding me continued until one Monday morning. Looking over the weekly calendar I realized the degree to which coaching had seemingly snuck up on me. My client base had grown to fill a surprising majority of the week. Sitting back in my desk chair I reflected on the unintentionality of developing a full-time coaching clientele'. This was overlaid by the positive shifts taking place in the lives of those with whom I worked. The easy flow I seemed to have in this new role had made it so deeply enjoyable that a significant pivot had taken place, with neither struggle or effort.

Coaching: The Rise and Resistance

Coaching came as a most natural addition to my professional repertoire. The personal benefits I'd reaped from my original four female mentors had demonstrated the countless rewards available from individualized advisership. Ergo, receiving coaching had become an integral component of my personal growth journey long before it grew into the giant industry it is today.

Having been a committed learner and devoted reader since my youth, a notable percentage of the books I'd consumed had been written by experts in the field of personal development. These informative texts packed my shelves for years prior to dominating the New York Times and Wall Street Journal bestseller lists. Being ahead of that curve often found me wandering into used bookstores and asking for their personal development section, to which I was always greeted with, "what's that?" Books of this genre had not yet become so prolific as to rate their own section.

It was a time when the majority of the public still thought of coaches as being all but exclusive to sports. So, let's take a moment to consider coaching as an essential element of life. Imagine Serena Williams deciding that, having achieved recognition as one of the top female athletes in the world, and even in the history of female sports that she no longer needed a coach. All the great professional speakers I've known have coaches, particularly those with their sights set on the illustrious TED stage. I've yet to meet a highly successful business leader who does not work with a coach. In some cases two to three coaches and a personal mentor, simultaneously. In spite of having spent years developing content, without my writing coaches this book would, quite probably, still be stored on my laptop, in pieces.

What women are willing to give themselves in terms of high-level coaching speaks directly to how strongly they respect themselves, their capabilities and their intrinsic value. Years ago, I offered the timeworn excuse, "that's more than I can afford" to someone who ultimately became a respected coach. The reply rang as a loud wake-up call. *"You'll become who you believe you have the ability to become. If you don't think you're worthy of the cost of high-level coaching, I'd agree that you shouldn't invest the money."* I'll readily admit that piece of hard truth hit me right in the gut. After reflection on whether I could decide to be worthy of the investment in me, I jumped in and never looked back. Since that time, I've had quite a few amazing coaches and valuable mentors. Attending weeklong and weekend seminars, delivered by powerful thought leaders, is a regular investment in myself. At this point it's impossible to imagine ever setting down the pursuit of more of my potential by accessing all available channels.

A younger woman recently asked me to share my best business tip for success. My response was a nugget that had once been given to me, *"Never be the smartest person in the room. That's not a business tip. It applies to all areas of your life, from professional influences to friends. Always align yourself with people smarter than you."* I followed this up with my own insight. *"And always have a coach or a mentor or both."*

As highlighted in the previous chapter, untold studies reveal that most women are disinclined to enlist individualized advisors. Something men from all levels of business, politics, and life do, with consistency and with notable results. The majority of this research focuses on professional women or female business owners. Yet, the same holds true for those outside the business world. Cost is the primary reason women cite for not engaging. On many occasions, I've heard a woman speak of how deeply she longs to excel in some specific area. Or, she might reveal the great dream she desires to fulfill. Concurrently, she balks at the suggestion of hiring a coach. Not just me, but any coach. There have been many conversations in which a woman insisted, *"There's no way that I can afford coaching,"* from atop her $400 shoes.

I do understand and empathize with this embedded and self-limiting belief system. It was reinforced in me until it was challenged in a way that was both pointedly direct and kind. This is what fuels my passion to help other women understand the incredible value that is gained through both mentoring and coaching.

Is the tradition of women denying themselves access to professional coaching and mentoring solely due to issues of self-value? Might it be a fear of discovering long-avoided truths about themselves? Or, do they distrust the coaching experience itself? Is fear of success an active component here? I suspect there are sufficient examples of each. Due to fewer women having worked with mentors or coaches, their lack of understanding around the process is likely another hindrance. Whether you are a seasoned mentee and recipient of coaching or a novice, a personal coach can become just the cheerleader that is needed. The right one can fill the support role of collaborating the how's and what's of bold next steps.

A Peek Behind the Coaching Curtain

Considering the huge market influx of individuals hanging out a 'Coaching' shingle, it is easy to understand the doubt and confusion. What is it? What will I gain? Is it right for me? How do I know which one to work with? What will be expected of me? And of course, how much is justified for what I will receive? These are not only reasonable questions, they are the exact questions anyone seeking a coach is well served to consider. How can a woman unfamiliar with being on the receiving end appraise its importance, its efficacy, and the means for identifying an ideal fit? How will she assess which type of coach is best suited to help her achieve her personal goals?

Let's take a defining look at coaching, what it is and how it can help up-level one's personal and professional life. A skilled coach helps you identify unrecognized ingenuity and talent, where you want to go, what you want to accomplish and how to get there.

To quote internationally respected coach Betty Lam,

> *"Coaching can take you to uncharted territories that you never thought you would go to."*

Anytime we develop accelerated patterns for learning versus being taught how to respond by rote, we win. To be able to learn from a coach, we must enter the experience with the curiosity to expand our self-awareness. Being sincerely vested in mastering new ways to apply ourselves, or achieve previously illusive outcomes, pre-equips us with a desire to learn. Bringing a willingness to look, without judgment, at our personal gaps and mistakes is empowering.

94

As Karen Ann Boise, ACC, BCC, Certified Confidence Coach, who has spent years developing programs for certifying as a coach at the collegiate level explains:

> *"You can have it, do it, be it and achieve it. This is the priceless result of working with a coach. Whether it is a personal goal or a career goal, working with a coach will not only help you get out of your own way but enable you to take the thoughts, dreams and desires out of your head and heart, lay them all out, look at them, examine them and if you so choose, take action to realize them. Coaches ask questions that can lead to the answers you hold within you. They act as a thought partner and can facilitate and engage in brainstorming and then work with you to create an action plan on how to move forward, when to move forward and then check in with you to hear about the outcome."*

Being an avid recipient of coaching is not limited to a single area or two of my life. Benefitting from the long-honed expertise of another in any area has helped me to realize broader personal expansion in condensed periods of time. Some of the professionals for which I am continually grateful are my fitness coach/personal trainer, business coach(s), wellness coach, public speaking coach, and writing coach. As with the example of Serena Williams, just because we have years of practice in an area doesn't mean there's not more to learn.

What Will Work for You

Identifying what type of coach and coaching will best drive your current vision to realization is a sound step toward meeting your best self and living your best life. While the majority of seasoned coaches will have the skills to address many areas of life or business, most have a specialty.

While there are unlimited fields of coaching, here are just a few of the more broadly recognized to consider for your own purposes.

Specialty Coaching

I have two colleagues, one in the US and the other in New Zealand providing exceptional Wellness Coaching. Both of these women are highly certified in a variety of areas, all related to wellness. Each has many years as a practitioner, a coach, and being coached. Additionally, these women have a list of happy clients, including myself, who have achieved vastly increased levels of health and overall fitness.

Another example of specialty coaching is Dr. Shelly Gruenig, who you will meet later in this chapter. Dr. Shelly has developed an internationally respected STEM team of young, school-age kids. Coaching is not just for adults. Sometimes it is the pathway to helping your kids discover their passion in life, from a very early age. Dr. Shelly, who was recently inducted into the STEM Hall of Fame and is ranked the #4 top STEM coach worldwide, brings vast knowledge to this role of how to support those she coaches and mentors to excel and expand beyond any previous limitation.

Life Coaching

While this is one of the more commonly recognized arenas of coaching, it provides far more than is generally imagined.

You can think of a Life Coach as an expert in navigating the day-to-day challenges. They support us through the little hurdles that might otherwise send us spinning at a moment's notice, or for extended periods. This can include challenges in your relationships, career, or family. A Life Coach will remain with you through the period of integrating the life-enhancing changes to become a new, confident, and more productive self. On other occasions, these are the professionals who become trusted advisors for extended time frames. One example is, helping parents maneuver through their kids uncomfortably challenging tween years.

Business Coaching

This type of coaching can provide powerful support in assisting you to clarify your vision. It can help you steer through the achievement of goals for your company or business. Business Coaches are experts in assisting you to align your professional goals with those of your personal life, thus creating a sustainable balance. These coaches also identify the gaps in your existing systems and help you develop more robust processes that are well-grounded for long-term success.

Leadership Coaching

Leadership Coaching helps the client uncover unrecognized strengths and finesse talents that are already present, but often dormant. Their fine-tuned sensibility for helping the client pinpoint weaknesses and evolving them into areas of expertise is extremely valuable. A skilled Leadership Coach will establish a system of accountability that supports quantifiable progress. Simultaneously, they educate the client on how to build a tradition of the same practices throughout their company or team.

Transformational Coaching

There are degrees to which this is similar to Life Coaching. The notable difference being that Life Coaching focuses on changing the actions of the client. Transformational Coaching helps the client change the way they envision themselves. By clarifying existing self-perceptions, the client is able to see *how* they created debilitating habitual behaviors. This opens the door to reset the old mindsets, thus developing new behavior patterns, which results in reorienting life shifts.

Finding an Ideal Fit

1. First, determine the area of life you want to address.
2. Select the style of coaching with the strongest potential for accomplishing your goal.

Creating these outlines prior to seeking a coach will help you single out the professional most likely to be an ideal fit.

I've met numerous individuals who never had a coach, simply because they didn't know how to find one. Then there are those whose feelings about coaching were tainted by having ended up on the wrong end of—"My sister has a friend who has a cousin who once met _____ ." (fill in the name of someone well known within the industry)

Thrive Global offers these practical tips to help you locate your ideal coach:

1. Stalk them online. Not in a creepy way, of course!

2. Have an initial conversation. Free introductory consult.

3. Talk to two or three coaches. Ask for references you can speak with.

4. Look beyond the price tag. You're worth it.

5. Check your heart and gut as well as your head.

6. Notice if you start to talk yourself out of it.

7. It's all about chemistry.

Working with a coach is a very personal decision, from to coach up or not, to who I will choose. I encourage you to take your time deciding, but to not let the choice linger on the shelf, ignored and gathering dust.

What We Learn as Coaches

I find unmatched fulfillment in witnessing others achieve beyond where they had previously dared to endeavor, and understanding that they can continue to fulfill any goal or desire. I cannot imagine a time when this would cease to be an enriching experience.

From the other side of the desk, throughout all the varied experiences of my life to date, nothing has taught me more about myself than offering Transformational Coaching to others. By the same token, I have encountered no clearer path for up-leveling my many and varied assets, than receiving coaching. Learning to weave my natural gifts into a single comprehensive expression is an exciting and fascinating journey. It is a rare experience that allows everyone to benefit in all directions.

Modern-day Mighty Woman: Dr. Shelly Gruenig

As mentioned, Dr. Shelly Gruenig was recently inducted into the STEM Hall of Fame and is ranked the #4 top STEM coach worldwide. Additionally, as she was building her STEM team she realized the importance of teaching Leadership at the same time. By teaching the older, more experienced kids, to pass their knowledge on to the younger ones in the program, Dr. Shelly is preparing the kids in her program to be prepared for multifaceted lives and careers.

Robots Took Over

Robots took over my life in 2005 as I was searching for something more to do in the way of science for my children. As a homeschool teacher with a PhD in Workforce Education, I wanted to ensure that my kids had career focus and real experiences in life to support their career decision-making. With those factors in mind, I stumbled upon the B.E.S.T. robotics competition and found the perfect opportunity for our family.

On that day in 2005 I knew nothing about robotics. As I sit here today, I am proud to say that has changed and the team I started for my own children now benefits thousands. The program has built students into 13- time champions, world competitors, STEM (Science, Technology, Engineering and Math) entrepreneurs and filled the STEM Workforce pipeline. Along the way, I have become an advocate and a thought leader in STEM enrichment and entrepreneurship.

From the beginning, the guiding principle of the program has always been to become a greater version of yourself through learning and fun. Perhaps because I was bullied as a child, it has been my mission to create a safe place for students to "find their people" and give them a place to thrive. To offer space where opportunities and dreams can be chased and achieved no matter who you are.

What I didn't realize when I established the program was that coaching a group of nerdy students would enable me to live out my own STEM dreams joined by a circle of women who were passionate about STEM.

Girl Powered

I will never forget the pride that I felt as our first girls only team competed for the first time ever. As the day came to a close and awards were announced, they were all surprised to receive the top award in the state. A team of young ladies who repeatedly thought about giving up on the journey because it was too hard, or they didn't "know enough". It was at that moment that I realized the full power of being an audacious mentor to young women. That by encouraging them to do hard things, and more importantly, to believe in themselves in a way I never did would change their lives and mine as well. As one student put it, "Less Pink, More Think".

To be surrounded by a circle of women supporting students as they develop their skills, face their fears, and challenge the thinking of others in order to build a better product, has changed not just them but me as well.

Radical Change

While coaching has brought about many small changes in my life, in 2014 it was the impetus for several epic life changes. Those radical changes in my life resulted in greater financial stability, a more positive mindset, and a much healthier body. Whether it is building a championship robotics program or making radical personal changes, I believe that if I can do it so can you! Simply step forward and get started because it is never too late to become a greater version of ourselves!

Of course, radical change isn't always easy. For students, I teach two principles that when applied, have helped me to achieve my goals. Those principles are first to Fail Forward and second to Be Greater. To Fail forward is to not to simply persevere, it is an attitude of welcoming challenges while remaining coachable. The principle of Be Greater comes from training yourself to innovate and set a plan to reach for dreams that build self-esteem while conquering what once seemed impossible.

Failing Forward

In competitive robotics, the engineering design process guides decisions and keeps a team moving forward as they reiterate. Each of the five steps, Investigate, Innovate, Collaborate, Create and Evaluate offer opportunities to learn through others as well as self-study. They also provide an unending amount of moments to problem solve and move forward, reiterating and "failing forward".

During my years as coach I can't count the number of times that failing forward led to struggles and challenges as well as the best moments ever whether in my own life or in the lives of the students I was working with.

Too often, we want to take the easy way rather than journey down the road less traveled where we will face challenges and fall. The difference in failing forward is that we choose to persevere and make a move to get up again. Sometimes that is done by gathering information, investing in ourselves, while other times it is by stepping aside and peering over the shoulder of an expert.

Perseverance

In 2011 the team had an amazing robot that was designed to climb a ten-foot pole. To score points, the robot had to climb the pole with gamefield pieces and then place them in bins at the top. It was a challenging competition and a week before at an organized practice day we had the only robot out of 24 teams that could score points.

Students were proud of their hard work and practiced nonstop, fully expecting to win the statewide competition.

Throughout that six-week season, I had noticed that they were using bolts without nuts, not screws, drilled into the plywood robot base. After questioning this decision a multitude of times and being assured that the bolts would hold, I relented. Competition day came and we were scheduled for six rounds with the robot. In the first round, the driver forgot the remote control...zero points. In the second round, just as the robot reached a foot off of the ground and things were looking good, all of the wires fell out because someone had forgotten to insert the small plastic wire clip...zero points. Finally, in our final round before lunch the robot was finally climbing the pole and poised to score. Suddenly, one of the bolts in the plywood base failed and sent the entire creation crashing to the ground. Chunks of the robot went flying and the entire stadium went silent in shock.

Three of the team members gave up their lunch to work frantically and make repairs on the robot, but it wasn't enough. At the end of the day, the team had barely gotten off the ground. Tears flowed. Students ran to find private spaces as they were filled with sadness over how their sure win had become an "epic failure".

Later that year, I would take a small group of the students to the TX BEST regional championships as volunteers rather than competitors. It was a powerful lesson for them that paid off two years later. The same group of students would work to win the very first Overall Regional Championship. I believe that without the loss and the opportunity to fail forward, that group of students would have never known that they could Be Greater. For me, it was a lesson that it is okay to embrace Texas sized epic failures, check your pride, pack up your fears and get back in the game on a journey to Be Greater.

Be Greater

While there are many opportunities in life to Be Greater and to journey from Learner to Leader, part of believing in yourself is standing up for what you believe in. For so many years I struggled with this concept, often thinking that it was selfish to believe in me. I became an expert at believing in others and empowering them to believe in themselves while unable to make the same investment in myself. Until Dereck joined the team.

Dereck spent many years in our program and as an Alumni he remains committed to the program. When he was just 15, he witnessed a bad call at the state competition. Rather than simply be angry and feel the injustice, he walked up to the judges table and challenged the decision of judges. These judges, PhD professors and industry professionals, were toe to toe with a student who struggled with dyslexia and ADHD. They had no idea of the effort it took him to learn to read the game rules. With tears flowing I stood and watched alongside his parents. We were witness to the courage it took, armed only with his own understanding of the competition rules that he had read to face the intimidating group.

Ultimately, the judges changed their decision to reflect the rule, but only after being courageously challenged by this student who was simply standing up for what was right....and he did this all for another team!

In this world, it is an important lesson to be able to speak up for oneself. To stand your ground and believe in your own truth is a powerful lesson that enables us to then act in compassion and believe in others. That lesson forced me to start standing up for me even when I didn't believe it. It taught me to employ the "As If" principle to open up my world and dream again.

Start Dreaming

Author Richard Wiseman writes that we can create our outer circumstances by acting "As-If" they are already real. While at first glance the principle may seem more magical than real, Wiseman explains the foundational evidence of the principle designed to help us innovate our own lives.

Put another way, author Napoleon Hill wrote, *"Whatever the mind can conceive and believe, it can achieve"* in his book Think and Grow Rich. In other words, to accomplish something begins first by believing you can.

Like the little train engine that could, young people have an amazing ability to dream about the future and believe in themselves. Whether it is the house they want to live in, the career they want to have, the places they will visit, or the kind of life they will live; kids can dream. As we grow, society teaches us to set aside dreams and take on responsibilities so that we can focus on "adulting".

What if I told you that was all a lie, and that by setting aside those dreams, you were really killing yourself? Most people can simply consider this and know it is true. When was the last time you felt alive and excited about life? I imagine it was at a time that you were living a dream or taking the time to consider a dream. So going forward, remind yourself to act "As If" and believe in yourself knowing that you can achieve anything the Good Lord helps you to conceive.

Crashing Champions

In 2014, I thought I was living a dream as we headed home after three days at the TX BEST Robotics regional championship competition. The team had put in a huge amount of effort, and it paid off exponentially. On the ride home, ten of us, all of our equipment and numerous trophies, awards, and prizes, including the First Place Overall Championship trophy that the students had won through hard work and determination, against more than 240 other teams from across the region.

In less than five minutes, a light rain turned to ice as the temperature plummeted, and we careened off the road followed by all of the vehicles following us. When we finally came to a stop, our caravan was on its side and the only way out was to climb up through the windows.

Together, this group of champions really earned their trophy as they cared for one another, helped nearby strangers, and overcame a really scary situation. These young people were truly Greater Than Average and proved it, on the side of the road and the challenging day we faced afterward to simply get home safely.

Processing the event in the following weeks required me to confront the fact that I had given up hope in my dreams, and that it is never too late to go running to them. In fact, it's not unusual to come to similar realizations when we are faced with near death experiences. I experienced the near death not just of myself, but of an entire group of people for whom I cared deeply and felt responsible. I smile now as I think of how I looked like a Jack in the box exiting the vehicle with the boost from my students. That boost was the jolt that I needed to be shocked back to life and live "As If", pursuing my dreams to Be Greater.

Chase Dreams

We do not need to wait for a near death experience to take action and chase down our dreams. After the accident, I began pursuing a dream of being on a crew for a hot air balloon team. The beauty of a sky filled with hot air balloons, which is a frequent occurrence in New Mexico, is awe-inspiring and helps me to believe and conceive. The days when together with my family we bundle up and wrap our hands around warm mugs of hot cocoa long before the sun rises to chase dreams create endless joy. As we unpack, lay out, inflate, launch, chase, land, and stow the beautiful hot air balloon, the beauty takes my breath away.

What is it that takes your breath away and helps rekindle some of your childlike joys and passions? You may begin by supporting the dreams of others, but it is never too late to join me in the journey of chasing down your dreams and living your best life.

My Biggest Fan

The call came in 2017 only two weeks following another state championship victory. I was sitting at the kitchen table, with dozens of students in the home and garage preparing for the TX BEST regional robotics championship. In a faraway voice, my stepdad shared that my mom had just died. All I could think was how could this be, we were just laughing on the phone only hours before. Mom had been in the stands at every competition since 2006 and was every student's robotics grandma. She kept a small photo album in her purse so that she could share the details with any stranger that would listen.

Following her death, the students had wanted to win in honor of her. Sadly, by the end of the day we had given up our dream of winning the overall award and I consoled myself that it was enough that we had even qualified to be there.

As we packed up all of our spirit banners and noisemakers, this first season without my mom cheering beside thousands in the stands, and all I wanted to do was leave. Pasting a smile on my face for the sake of the team, I told them to all gather at the far end of the stadium for one last team picture.

We reached our destination and I heard the announcer call our team name for an award. In a booming voice, the announcer said "Is R4Robotics even still here?" He didn't see us in our normal seating area.

As the students ran to spill onto the stadium floor, voices kept calling out *"What did we win?"* The founder of the competition ran up to me to congratulate the team, *"Congratulations on your First Place Championship - the biggest award of the competition".*

Hope Restored

Astonished, I turned to see that the students had accepted the large trophy and were arranging themselves for a photo. In that sweet moment, I realized that hope had been restored and that their As If had come true. I was overcome with joy for them and the thought of it still causes tears to flow due to the lesson that even in dark times, when we alone have given up hope, it still exists.

That win in 2018 not only restored my hope, but it helped to remind me that I needed to be willing to take on my own fears. To pack them up and get in the game of life embracing my failures as lessons and the wins as opportunities. To start living your best life and start dreaming again, you must first believe that you are worth it.

The lessons that I have learned as a mentor and coach of a robotics team have helped me to break free from the prison of my own mind and the fears that lock the cell. Watching the students, including my own children, has been one of the greatest blessings of my life.

Helping them to find their people has opened doors for me to role model tackling challenges, problem solving, advocating and doing hard things even when I didn't believe in myself.

In the end, the program I founded to help others has helped me more. The rewards of mentoring and helping place students into careers while working with businesses across the country have been too numerous to count. Learning to be a STEM entrepreneur, facing challenging situations and disappointed students as well as my own demons and fears while surrounding myself with a STEM sisterhood have helped me to create and pursue new dreams.

To Fail Forward and Be Greater in their pursuit of launching their lives has indeed helped me to find my own greatness that was once hidden inside of me, but now shines for the world to see.

Hard Seasons Pay Off

In 2020 my youngest daughter graduated and I faced one of the hardest seasons of life. Amid a worldwide pandemic, I was facing a personal transition that was harder than I could have imagined. At the same time, I wondered if I would be capable of ensuring the robotics program would be sustainable and a part of the community to provide opportunities for my grandchildren.

During that difficult time, the years of acting "As If" began to pay dividends. Alumni wrote posts about their powerful experiences, students came up with an idea to use their STEM skills to fill the need for face shields to the tune of 3D printing nearly 6,000 shields all while parents, government officials and business owners stepped up to ask how they could help grow our impact.

The funny thing is, if you would have told this inexperienced mom back in 2005 that the team that only scored one point (by accident) would become State, Regional, and International award winners, I most certainly would have laughed at you. If you would have told my circle of STEM sisters back in 2005 that our program would one day serve tens of thousands of students, their families and educators, I know we would have not believed you (mainly because we were trying to put out the fire we started at my kitchen table while showing our kids how to make an electromagnet).

Thanks to mentoring and the power of amazing mentors of my own, I now know that the opportunities are endless and the key to unlocking my greatness is to look inward. Then, get busy failing forward, one epic fail at a time because it is never too late to stand up and join the journey to *Be Greater Than Average.*

Part Two

Chapter Seven

"We have to dare to be ourselves, however frightening or strange that self may prove to be."

~ May Sarton

HIDING IN PLAIN SIGHT

D
ue to my lifelong commitment to hiding in plain sight, becoming a professional speaker never crossed my mind. That was until I found myself unexpectedly thrust onto a speaking stage in my early 30's, as the last minute replacement for someone who had developed laryngitis. Fortunately, the event centered around a topic on which I was well versed. To this day I remain convinced it was the suddenness of that experience combined with the runaway pumping of my heart, terrified of dying up there, that allowed me to open my mouth and let words spill out.

Despite my initial reluctance...well if we're to call it what it was...terror...speaking to groups turned out to be a life that suited me. As shortly as five minutes after coming off that first stage I could not have told you a word I'd said. Yet, there was a magic in those moments of knowing I'd found a home, one I loved so completely that I've stayed for some 30+ years. Nevertheless, for a time the old programming and anxieties still rendered me incapable of allowing myself to be too seen, too heard, too recognized. Finding a place that fit like nothing I'd ever known did not magically dissolve the negative self-imaging I'd carried since youth. The gifts that gave me the courage to dive into this life with full vigor were the microphones, lecterns, and publicists that stood between me and everyone else. The simple distance from the stage to the audience seating also helped. Each of these felt like welcome, protective buffers. They allowed the gaping holes in my self-esteem overlaid on my introverted nature, to relax.

Having lived a bookish life, I didn't lack the knowledge or the skills to speak intelligently on the topic of the day. However, all my years of hiding between those pages had turned me into an armchair intellectual which only served to enhance my introversion. To this day, nothing has thrilled me more than long days spent sitting within a group, waxing-on philosophical, always with people brighter and more educated than myself. So, I was a nervous wreck about my ability to be the single person upfront. My constant prayer was to deliver something that was interesting and contributed value to the lives of others'.

A surprising discovery was that I possessed a natural capacity for storytelling. The ability to engage people by making them laugh was a saving grace that allowed me to have fun. The dividers standing between me and *them* gave me the courage and permission to keep going. Experiencing the thrill of watching a new light switch on in the eyes of someone in the audience was my prevailing motivation.

It was an exciting time filled with new environments to explore and people of different cultural origins, religions, spiritual and political views. Each of these offered a contrasting and fascinating perspective. Every place I visited invited me to view life through a new lens. Speaking became my passport into new worlds. I ultimately traveled throughout the U.S., from one side of Canada to the other and all the way down to Australia and New Zealand. My gypsy-spirit had never been happier. From Maori celebrations in New Zealand to eating catfish deep into the Louisiana bayou, the generosity of my sponsor's was humbling. I was introduced to sacred traditions, incredible environments, and one of my favorite indulgences, new foods. My fascination with human behavior was continuously fueled. Enchanted with the varying cultures, architecture, art, music, food, and the wonders of the natural world, life was full. And yet, in spite of how much I was enjoying all the many aspects of my adventures, it never ceased to feel like it was what I was doing until...Until...what?

Until What...

With that never-ending question echoing through the chambers of my mind, these were busy years. Being a speaker and sincerely comfortable with my perpetually single life allowed me the freedom to move at will, and I did. For one period of about a decade and a half I moved as regularly as some people go on vacation. Many within my worldwide network of friends joked about my 'entire page of addresses' in their pre-smart phone/phone books. All this served to conceal my utter discomfort. No one was allowed to get close enough to *really* know me, to realize how 'not quite' I was. Afterall, my stay was always going to be stamped with an expiration date. It was the life of, one-part seeker of something indefinable, one-part curious student, and one-part aspiring philosopher. I approached this lifestyle as one thrilling and extended education, with built-in escape hatches.

It was during these same years that I became fascinated with the idea of business. At the end of the day, I'd built and either crashed or sold several small businesses. With each success came the question, "What next?" Each crash brought the old self-recrimination bounding back to the surface. I wasn't yet at the point of noticing the pattern. Success, no time for self-congratulations or even a relaxing free weekend. Onward! Immediately! Only after a crash could I dally. And just long enough to lick my wounds and regurgitate my failings while wallowing in the mess.

With all this going on, the question of what I was *really* going to do lingered. How was I going to follow that placeholder of public speaking and small business dabbling? The truth was that deep inside I knew the answer. I'd known it since I was twelve years old when I'd had a dream. One that would revisit throughout my life and that, even at the time of it's happening, felt like a life mission, a purpose for being.

Sheltered by the shade of the giant tree in my parent's front yard, I was deep in focus, busily scribbling notes as quickly as my young hand would travel the paper. The dream had come the night before. One so deep and true that the sensation of that afternoon's heat, my cut-off shorts and little white cotton shirt with its red piping travel through time all the way to this current moment.

Oh, how many times I've wished I still had that little twelve-year-old girl's notes of all that would be required to make her dream a reality. No doubt, rooted in sweet innocence and naiveté. Regardless, that was the day my vision of facilitating a means for women to come together was born. The dream of being surrounded by women uplifting one another was branded in every level of my memory and cell of my body. Despite that image from age 12 never fading, the trust in myself and my abilities to create such a vehicle remained tightly locked away.

Sudden Changes

As the years passed, I began to nervously contemplate that I must have driven right past the corner, missing that last, and all-important turn. I had overlooked the indicators that would have directed my feet toward this long-imagined life purpose. Into my late fifties I was feeling a great thirst for a momentous change, even if I was still unsure what that would look like. Then, in a way I would have never chosen, couldn't have possibly imagined, in one single, fleeting moment, life made the choice for me.

Dashing into a grocery store during a rain spurt, I hit the wet floor not protected by rain mats and flew immediately skyward. The result was a hairline fracture and six torn ligaments down my spine, a severe concussion and whiplash. Three months later I was able to get out of bed without holding onto the chair I had placed beside it. Following another three and a half years spent in multiple forms of physical therapy I was sufficiently recovered to have the attention span to panic. Public speaking had gone into an indefinite holding pattern. When it's a struggle to simply get out of bed to get yourself to physical therapy there's no more running from this city to that country. With skyrocketing medical bills and an inability to work yet, I was broken from the inside out. I had no idea what I was going to do when I was fully mobile. Nothing makes a speaker irrelevant faster than disappearing from the face of the earth for three+ years. I was living on a thin thread between mental, emotional panic and continuing physical pain.

Never Too Late

Gifts from the universe are funny things. They can show up at the most unexpected times and places. Sometimes their arrival initiates an effect similar to a waterfall. We each receive them in a variety of forms throughout our lives. All too often a small amount of thought may be invested in them. Having not deciphered a precise meaning they are dismissed out-of-hand. With that brush-off, the gift they were offering is misplaced, at least for that moment.

This particular occasion rang clearly enough to ensure that it captured my full attention. While showering one morning I heard the words, *never too late* as clearly as if someone had walked into the bathroom and spoken them out loud. Without a moment's pause I was filled with excitement at knowing that whatever my *next* was going to be, this was its genesis. If I hadn't been afraid of slipping and falling again on the wet shower floor, I'd have done a happy dance right then and there. I'd long-since learned to pay attention to such messages and every sensation running through my cells said this was about women standing in alliance.

The following two years were a flurry of activity that included several false starts in bringing my *next* to life. Fortunately, my years of building small businesses had fortified me against throwing my hands and plans in the air. Walking away when plan A, B or even C didn't work out as imagined, never achieved anything. More recently, my ever-reliable tenacity had gotten me up after my physical and metaphoric fall and grit had become a steadfast friend.

Hundreds of interviews with women ensued. We discussed their unfulfilled dreams. Some shared their sense of emptiness at not having a personal dream. We talked about how to identify the indicators confirming that they were on the best path. We masterminded how to know when they had lost the thread and what to do to reconnect with it. Most let me ask why they had not dared to chase their dream. When did they realize they had let it go? Would they be just as satisfied with their lives if they permanently shelved the vision? What was the tipping point that had provoked them to put it all on the line to pursue their own *next*? Did they have an established support network of both cheerleaders and advisors? If not, what was their strategy for creating one? We discussed everything that women do and many things they too often hold in secret. I spoke with women who were adamant about not liking other women, refusing to work with them when it could be avoided. Then there were the women who had been on the receiving end of those judgments and incivilities. They found themselves feeling timid around other women for fear of a repeat, while quietly longing for those alliances. There were the hesitant women and the ones who shared secrets they'd never spoken out loud. Regardless of their story, I was honored by the trust expressed as they shared from a deeply personal place.

It quickly became clear the perspectives being offered were the beginning of a book. But what that would look like had not yet congealed. I imagined it had, but such is the way of projects during their inception period. Learning to be gentle with ourselves while the larger picture comes into frame is a journey unto itself for most women. Coming to peace with this was the secondary gift in my burgeoning *next* undertaking. Also, letting these big projects rest lightly in our hands while showing us what they will evolve into is a necessary application of patience. This is what reveals the passageway through the transformation we must navigate to develop into a good shepherd. Only then can our vision materialize into its fullest potency. If we'd previously been ready, it would have already come into being.

With so many ideas running through my mind, like a hamster on a wheel, it felt like time to share what I was doing with two friends. I'd previously found each to be adept sounding boards. There is a long-standing school of thought that says, keep what you are doing to yourself. This is generally sound advice, particularly during initial stages. Yet, there does come a moment when wisdom suggests that we speak with a trusted advisor. This can save tremendous work and energy otherwise spent backtracking and reworking our strategy.

Big life shifts are funny in how they evolve. If we stay the not yet clearly defined course the details will reveal themselves. During lunch with one of the business savvy friends I'd chosen to consult, a far broader image began to take shape. With eyes closed he listened attentively to my story from its shower-soaked inception. I walked him through the interviews, to the body of new female alliances and colleagues I had been developing. With my conclusion he excitedly proposed, *"This needs to be a book and a TED Talk! I know just the person to help you make that happen."* Texts flew back and forth, followed by a Zoom introduction and my *next* had made its way into *now*!

I'd like to say that having accomplished all I had in preparation for this step it was a smooth sail forward. Transparency demands I confess that this was when the hardest uphill trudge began. Equally, the coach and mentor in me wants to tell you that although this phase can sometimes feel overwhelming, *"Don't quit! You may need to take a designated break period. But make sure it's stamped with an expiration date and when you don't feel like you're ready to restart, and you may well not, do it anyway! Or else, your limbic system will convince you to just wait a little longer. This is the point at which you risk never restarting."*

Am I saying that from the time of that Zoom introduction I jumped on the horse and rode it all the way through the yellow ribbon of victory at the finish line? Yes. Through every false start, full stop, leaping too many hurdles to recount, circling around the barn, back out to leap the burning bushes, sloshing through the deep bogs, wailing through every melt-down, pacing bare places in the carpet, wearing out sheets by tossing and turning while endless words tumbled through my sleepless mind, writing, deleting, writing more, tossing it all in the trash, writing again, I did. It doesn't matter if your dream is a book or any other expression of your passion. The only way through the untamed ego's suppression that has held it at bay until now, is to meet it face on and audaciously keep going.

Modern-day Mighty Woman: Anne Sermons Gillis

Anne Sermons Gillis is an internationally respected speaker, spiritual life coach, interfaith minister and advocate for affirming the truth in all religions, faiths, and spiritual traditions.

Being Broken is Natural

I am relatively accomplished. I am the author of five books, I have traveled the world, and I have gone for the gusto. I have been a role model for some, a mentor to others, and even envied by a few. My accomplishment list is long, but my failure list is longer. Tough times come, but through some fortunate twist of fate or perhaps due to my personal tenacity, I learned to stand tall even through emotionally crippling times. Being broken is natural, but not letting our light shine, despite our brokenness, is a tragedy.

Let me back up a bit and tell my story. In 1984, I joined with two other women to form a holistic counseling center. The word "holistic," in the south, was somewhat a cross between a pejorative and an incantation. No one had heard of the word, and in a straight-laced, conventional town, such as Memphis, Tennessee, our motives were suspect. Would we bring turmoil and dissension to the graciousness of the deep south?

Have I let the cat out of the bag? Yes, I am a rebel. I rebelled relatively early on. I was raised in the 50's. When I reached 19, I married and dutifully fulfilled my role as a wife. I was full of passion for everything, but given my station in life, I became the consummate homemaker. That was the only place to rightfully share my creativity. I did such a good job that our friends were hesitant to invite my husband and me to dinner. My dinner parties were lavish; so epicurean that my husband begged me to stop. "You make others feel inadequate." *Little did he know, and neither did I, that when there is greatness inside, it must come out, even if it has nowhere else to land other than at the dinner table.* Let me make this clear. I do not consider myself special. I believe that greatness lives in everyone, and that greatness, this sweetness, moves in and through us. And it will find a way out. Our life force will express itself, whether it be as an IT genius or through imaginative doodling.

Unfortunately, women have been relegated to the back seat of greatness. Our curiosity has been called obstinance. Our strength has been labeled anger, and our passion judged as hysteria. Even making a helpful suggestion is seen as micromanagement, by our men, who never worked through their mommy issues. When we speak out about an injustice, we are told to calm down. Women need a place to openly express how difficult it is to live in a man's world. This is only one of the reasons having female friends is invaluable. They help us move our power into a space and place of honor.

To give you an idea of how habituated I was to sex role scripting, even as I began my journey of empowerment, consider this. A male friend looked at my home office one day, saw my scattered research papers, and mentioned that I needed a filing cabinet. I was shocked at the suggestion; only important people had filing cabinets. Only real businesspeople were important, and those people were always men. Can you believe it? I grew up in a time where women believed themselves inferior to men and in a culture that never questioned that decision.

Still, there was this spark, and, like many women, I was too curious, too inquisitive to live within the confines of societal expectation. I meditated, read, analyzed, and pleaded, to no end. I saw two choices: I could give up or give in. I decided to give in. I would give in to that which was greater than I, even if I had no idea what that was. One desperate night, I gave it all up, and something happened. I could see in a way I had never seen before. It was as if a veil lifted, and I realized that the amazing life I was finally seeing had always been present. Why hadn't I noticed? The beauty, the pleasure of life, was present all the time. While this glimpse of heaven on earth did not cure the ills of my life, it provided a life raft. I no longer felt like I was constantly drowning.

Now I was a radiant light who held hands with, and sometimes even clutched, the hands of limits, fear, and shame. I dropped out of college when I got married, but, at the ripe old age of 26, returned to school. I thought I was old and washed up, but school returned me to a place where dreams were born. I took women's studies, and the more I saw strong women, female professors, women scholars, and learned about the injustices to women, the angrier I became. I was suffocated by a culture where I felt like a second-class citizen. I not only became a feminist and joined NOW; I went off the deep end. I wanted to be strong, independent, and self-sufficient. I carried my own boxes, real and metaphorical, and thought if I took help from anyone, it would be a show of weakness. I became a super man in a woman's body. My sister, who was ten years my senior, rescued me with her words of wisdom, "Let them carry the boxes. Let men do the heavy lifting. It is a gift you give them. They love to do that. You seek interdependence, not anti-dependence."

Ultimately, though I softened a tad, I succeeded in a man's world. I found it quite austere. Some people might love living at the top, but there, on the steep point of that mountain, there was no place to relax, no room for others, and no time for magic. The other side of darkness and oppression was darkness and oppression. Women were objectified, but so were men. Men were just in a different kind of trap. That was what the women's movement was about – liberation for all. When women were liberated, men were liberated too. Unfortunately, only a few men yearned for liberation. They were comfortable at the top of the mountain, even if they had forsaken themselves.

I divorced during my final college semester and entered a time of emancipation, though I did not travel a clear path. I stumbled and fell, repeatedly, but I took my magic with me, even through the bowels of hell. I might have had demons to fight. I might not have been the most brilliant woman alive, but I was me, and no matter what, I marched on. I remarried too soon, to a person who made my first husband look like Prince Charming. I was still under the illusion that having a man in my life would solve the existential problem of being me. I divorced again and meandered through a string of delightfully unhealthy relationships. The curriculum of relationships is rigorous, and the more pain and angst I felt, the more I stripped away my neediness, feelings of abandonment, and shallowness. I learned to walk into a business meeting with my guts temporarily stuffed into my pants suit. My craziness, fear, and soaring anxiety did not need to be a roadblock. They could be stepping stones.

Back to the counseling center, which by now had blossomed into an alternative spiritual center we called Connection. My fiancé of several years walked into the arms of another woman. I was devastated. At the time of the breakup, which stretched on for months, I saw clients though I felt insane. I was teetering on the edge of despair; each moment disappointed me, but during it all, I remained a competent therapist. I would hop into my colleague's office before I had a client and ask, "How do I look? Do I look like a screaming meemie or do I look normal? Can you tell?" She smiled, "No, you can't tell. You look fine." One word from a trusted friend and colleague empowered me. I would walk into my office and sit with my client. I was strong in my compassion and steadfast in my support of their dilemma. It was eerie how my clients' problems reflected my woes. The universe sent women who were going through painful breakups. Fortunately, I was one step in front of them, and I taught them my coping skills. No one thought about how bad I looked because they looked worse. I taught them how to make the impossible possible. These ideas helped us all:

Do not jeopardize your job because of a breakup. Do not cry at work. If you are triggered and must cry, go to the bathroom to recover. Speak to yourself. Tell yourself that you can grieve and fall apart, but that you must wait until you return home to collapse. You do not have to grieve 24 hours a day. Make good on your promise when you get home and give yourself the space to grieve.

Do not miss work. This helps you. Your work will structure your time so that you can take a break from your pain.

When you feel wretched, call a friend. Give them the scoop. "I am in pain. I need your support. Is this a good time to talk?" If they say yes, ask them to tell you what they like about you. If you call one person and they are not at home, call until you find someone to support you. *Get immediate support.* Tell your friend you do not need fixing; you only need love, compassion, and presence. "Hold my hand. Walk with me in my pain. Do not try to fix me, change me, or solve my problems." People often approach emotional problems with intellectual solutions. When they start offering solutions, we may find ourselves in the awkward position of saying. *"Yes, but."* When we teach others how to give the support we need, they usually rise to the task.

Borrow courage from others. There is nothing like reading how others have made it through a difficult time or drawing from a friend's courage. I have a friend whose 12-year-old son was killed in a gun accident. It was hard to deal with, but she did what she could to muddle through. Then another tragedy struck. Her home flooded, and her unemployed husband had not paid the flood insurance. They moved into another home, paid rent, and continued to pay the mortgage on the flooded home, which was never rebuilt, until it was paid off. Her husband and mother became ill, and she cared for them both until they passed away, within weeks of each other. She was in her mid-seventies when we met, and she was still working long hours. Her circumstances had not allowed her to save money for retirement, yet she was upbeat. While I do not want to diminish my challenges, I draw strength and courage when I see what others have come through and how they stand in their power during the dark times. Despite all of my friend's tragedies, she never gave up. She used positive thinking to move her from the hole she might have remained in if she had not climbed out of her circumstances. She might not have flown during those times, but she was still standing. She paid bills, worked, and even found peace in her daily life. Giving up was not an option.

Write it out. Journaling, for me, is like having a personal mental health professional at my fingertips. I always have an "It Sucks" journal. maybe you would like an "It Sucks" journal. Write down three things a day, more if necessary, that sucked during the day, or even things that happened in the past that still bother you. Someone would not let you in traffic. You stumped your toe. You were disappointed because someone ate the pizza slice you were going to eat for breakfast. Speaking the truth does not make us negative people; it makes us emotionally gifted people. Writing it down is a way to let off steam. After writing down the complaints or disappointments, cross though each line and sign, "Paid in full." This means you do not have to carry it around. If you cannot let it go, put it on tomorrow's list, but ask your higher Power to help you let go of the upset around the incident. Keep it on your daily list until your upset dissipates, but remember, mark it off your list every day. If we have always been bright, cheerful, and a bit too "good," our shadow probably needs a bit of room to be negative, so our heavy emotions do not creep back in through the back door.

We moved from Texas to South Carolina in 2020. I call it my "trifuckta year." On the drive from Texas, I was in a head on collision that totaled my car. Due to COVID, I did not want to go to the Dublin, Georgia hospital. But during the night I was in such pain, my husband drove me, in our truck, to the ER. Though I was sore and banged up, the doctor announced that I had no broken bones, but there was an area of concern. The MRI showed what looked like cancer on my kidney. The next day my daughter picked me up, along with what was left of the contents of the car, and drove me to SC. My husband drove our packed truck and we settled down in our RV. We had a major problem getting my insurance changed from Texas to South Carolina, especially since Social Security offices were closed. It was like the world was in a standstill due to COVID and making changes to our lives was not an option. After hours spent daily on the phone, and time in bed recovering, everything was in place for me to have a partial nephrectomy. I had the surgery, and we moved from our RV, which we lived in for five months, six weeks after surgery, into our new home. Through all the trials and pain of my personal trifuckta, COVID, car crash, and cancer, I must say, I made it fine. I had many calls from friends, cards, and flowers. It made a difference. They carried my heart and kept it safe while I traversed the realms of not knowing, endured physical pain, and had to depend on others to care for me.

Recently, while unpacking, I found a letter from a friend who attended Connection. She wrote, in glowing terms, about the talk I gave one Sunday morning. I read with rapt attention, resting, glowing in her words. She purchased the cassette of the talk and listened repeatedly. She shared copies with friends. Then I came to the real kicker: she said that the most important part was when I said I was standing in my power, even as I navigated my abandonment issues. Her words reminded me of the truth. Sharing our vulnerabilities and our lower nature requires courage. It demands that we take risks. "Suppose they do not like me when they find out I am not invincible?" But self-disclosure usually has the opposite effect. Exposing our weaknesses to others inspires people as much as sharing our success stories and our *against all odds* stories. Her letter speaks to the power we have when our strength stands beside our shame. It transforms our weaknesses into stories, lessons, and realizations. We are not perfect, nor can we escape the limits of the human form, but if we courageously face our limits, we charge our spiritual momentum, and our lives become easier and safer.

There is something sturdy about life that holds us and pumps courage into us during our darkest moments. I almost feel embarrassed that I could have gone through so much, yet the core of me was always strong. It was like, "You should be more upset, Anne. You are in denial!" But I was not. We can be powerful women, even as we go through the worst of times. We are a tough and resilient group, and even when we stare death in the face, we can stand our ground. Women are not strong like oak trees, that snap in the wind; we are strong like a willow, that bends and lives long after the storm. When we carry the essence of who we are and stand firmly in the now, we can stand in our power, regardless of what goes on around us. Women are the voice of love, compassion, comfort, and power, and when it comes to our lives, we can *always* make them work.

Chapter Eight

"A crazy thing happened — the very act of doing the thing that scared me undid the fear. It's amazing the power of one word. 'Yes' changed my life. 'Yes' changed me."

~ Shonda Rhimes, writer, American television producer

RELUCTANT LEADERSHIP

More women than not have a secret space tucked away deep inside for those, 'maybe someday' desires. A more apt label for the majority might be, 'things I'll long for that will never come to pass.' Whether it's a level of business success, stepping into social advocacy leadership, developing a philanthropic organization, or running for office, their dreams remain just that. And these secret aspirations are not limited to professional undertakings. I can't count the number of women who have told me about that book they are going to write *someday*. There are the trips around the world they have been planning for years into decades or the sculpting classes they are going to pursue, *when*. Reluctance to step into their power, discover their potential for leadership, endeavor into the unknown and untried, is a woman's story as old as time. This is not to point fingers. Rather it is the naming of a truth known to all too many women. It is also an invitation for them to know that there are countless others out there playing the same self-withholding game. Untold numbers of women hold ambitions they have either never spoken out loud or always held just out of their own reach.

I spent more years than are helpful to dwell on working diligently to ride what I labeled, 'the radar's fine line'. The goal being to never drop very far below, lest I sacrifice too much of my physical comfort. Equally important was never rising too far above, for fear of being cast into a primary line of sight. The radar's fine line gave me the comfort of hiding behind the veils created by my fear, shame and failing self-image. Simultaneously, it let me support myself, engage in mentally and emotionally stimulating arenas, and travel around the world while remaining unseen, to any full extent.

Caught between the self-limiting beliefs that compelled me to hide and a natural ability to ascend with the speed of a cork rising in water, life felt like a dizzying roller coaster. As the speaking, mentoring and coaching engagements multiplied so did the number of women I was encountering. It was a revelatory time. These environments provided a safe space for one woman after another to reveal how they consciously stretch toward their own safe, unseen place. The majority shared stories of loneliness and frustration around their visions remaining unrealized. Others listed all the other people, situations, and traditions that held them back from their dreams, citing their annoyance and frustration with each. Other moments saw women revealing an unwillingness to work in situations that, while uncomfortable, would have supported their aspirations. There were women who had partnered and become mothers to avoid the fear that comes with being vulnerable enough to rise out of hiding. Some spoke in bold, adamant voices of their willingness to manifest their visions, but the gaps in their daily lives and professional satisfaction told a different tale. What was consistent throughout, was that none wanted to acknowledge the self-denial they were applying in order to deny themselves fulfillment.

Witnessing others strategies for dodging and hiding from overt leadership was an enlightening insight to my own. Stories I'd savored were expressed. My own favorite excuses were each exposed and always through the voices of women less unlike myself than was frequently comfortable to acknowledge. The most intriguing aspect of this was the way it made their brilliance so clearly visible. Their unique and creative approaches to maintaining this dance were seemingly limitless. But then that makes perfect sense. From girlhood most women have their personal identities tempered at best, and all-too-often completely stolen. What can't be taken are the still quiet voices calling up from their depths, striving to remind them of the *more* that they each are. I danced around the radar's fine line while living a life that satisfied me beyond anything I'd previously experienced. All the while I kept that line well within sight to assure that I didn't stray too far from its imagined safety. The women I met each had their own and equally inventive approaches to soul survival.

Whether through books, friends, professional support vehicles or classes, women need help highlighting those clear indicators of self-limitation. Increasing numbers are giving themselves permission to accept directional encouragement. Clarifying where we are deceiving ourselves is significant for course-correcting into new behavior patterns. Too often the very idea of this unnerves us, even when it's a shift we've been long craving.

Often the first and greatest concern the majority expressed was that if they changed, all their existing relationships would fall away. Those courageous enough to take a chance on themselves discover that they first expand their support system by adding new, intentionally uplifting connections. When some do fall away, instead of a deep wrenching, it comes as a natural evolution. The former friend falls off the frequently called list, with barely a notice. Realization of having simply outgrown them comes gently, and sometimes with great relief. Just as was experienced with friends from many different phases of life, with whom there is no longer, or only an infrequent connection.

Unpaid Labor: The Cost on Women's Lives and Ambitions

The most common self-inflicted restriction I see women accessing is avoidance. They work to maintain their focus on anything that helps to sidestep acknowledging that they are amazing beyond their wildest imaginations. Take a moment, set this book down in your lap. Close your eyes, and consider everything you address each day, week, month, and year. Start from the moment you open your eyes and run through the commitments of a typical day, until you close them again at night.

Partnered or not, there are the needs of both the house and the home, for they are different things. Maybe there are kids, grandkids, or aging elders. Dr's appointments, extracurricular activities, groceries, food preparation, laundry, dry cleaning to drop off and then pick up, the car maintenance, bills to pay, and following this incomplete list we haven't yet included work outside of the home. If partnered, it is important to find time within all of this for intimate moments and date nights. If not, there is (hopefully) a vibrant social life.

The issue of women's unpaid labor is a significant roadblock to finding space in their lives to pursue leadership roles. Feeling they can find the time and energy to effectively take these on, is a legitimate concern. If women were paid a mere minimum wage for the unpaid labor they do around the house and caring for family, present and extended, as a collective they would have made $1.5 trillion last year. That exceeds the combined earnings of the top fifty companies in the world. It is also based on our current minimum wage rate, which in no way resembles a living wage.

Women possess untold skills, those passed through their genetic lines as well as what they learned from elder females throughout their early years. From the time a girl child is born she is taught to be resourceful, creative, resilient, innovative, and far more responsible for everyone around her than what is either fair or realistic. The task list of what a woman accomplishes during a typical week, month, year, does not factor in the skills required to accomplish this most effectively. When considering the issue of unpaid labor these highly developed skills are often lost. Is it any wonder so many women find the idea of leadership to be daunting?

Reluctant Leaders

The awareness that women often say they're not ready to accept a power role, while men never do, has led to great misconceptions. One of those is based on study results revealing that women are less likely to hang their ego on the next big promotion or being awarded the ever-famous corner office. This has developed into a misunderstanding that they don't enjoy that status. The truth is that they do. They simply don't base their entire self-value on it.

Additional studies reveal that some women are not comfortable taking themselves seriously under the banner of 'Leader'. For many women, this is not rooted in their desire to play small. Rather it expresses a distaste for the way in which this title has been used by men as a platform for domination over subordinates, versus empowerment of team members. Former general counsel for the Department of Defense, Jamie Gorelick has said,

> *"The dirty little secret is that women demand a lot more satisfaction in their lives than men do."*

This observation returns our attention to the burden of the unpaid labor for which women are held responsible. Their broader range of responsibilities, apart from the workplace, provides a more comprehensive lens through which they view their lives. All this contributes to the assumption that many women are reluctant leaders. Stepping beyond this stereotyping, let's consider why women's additional personal requirements for taking on leadership roles make them ideal candidates.

Years of on-the-job training in the organizational skills necessary to manage a house, home, family, and all that entails, while also working outside the home, has taught women to get things done in the most fluid and time-effective manner. Due to everything women handle for the whole family in terms of dealing with authorities at their kid's schools, insurance professionals, medical professionals, and the overpriced plumber, they have up leveled their communication skills to a point of excellence. Consider the mother of a teenager, particularly a daughter committed to wearing the prom dress with a neckline plunging below the waist, versus what that mother feels is appropriate. What this woman knows about the art of negotiation, especially when the stakes are at their highest, could leave argumentative board members speechless.

Women are not reluctant to ascend to leadership, they simply require more motivation, in the form of greater appreciation for their uniquely effective styles.

Women's Unique Application of Power

With no intention to further victimize the injured parties in these scenarios, the question, *"Do women want power"*, is completely rational. It's been almost a decade since Patricia Sellers published an article in Fortune titled. *"Power: Do Women Really Want It."* I remember the furor that rippled through circles of feminists and women who were fighting vigorously for their right to be taken seriously by C-Suites, company, and organizational boards. All this time later, I still know women who lack the desire for the responsibility that comes with power. Some clearly state they simply don't have the additional bandwidth for it. Others speak openly of their distaste for the very word. Endless conversations reveal that often this is less a dismissal of a position than it is a rejection of the old patriarchal application of the word and its associated burdens.

How men execute power is vastly different from women's application. Women have long known that there is no physiological difference in men and women's abilities to be highly effective in positions of leadership. At this point, science has validated this as being unquestionable. What is equally apparent is that the difference rests in the emotional fabric of the sexes. Due to this uniqueness, women were disparaged as being too emotional to lead or balance power. As most women know, having these antiquated thought patterns projected on them has not yet taken its rightful place in ancient history. Instead, it continues to wield influence that sees women rejected for senior positions and board seats. All the while this fosters competition among women for the meager places that are made available at the table.

It's not a question of whether, or not women *want* power. The invitation is to understand the ways females express it uniquely and use it differently. Women don't typically view power as a possession to hold close for the purpose of using it to accumulate more in every direction. Their natural inclination is to examine it through a more holistic lens. What can it accomplish? Who and how can it serve? What can it build that is more than the sums of its parts? Furthermore, women are prone to pass the status it will give them forward to others. They inherently understand the additional influence that passing the torch generates. Growing numbers of women are leaving top level positions. They are bankrolling their influence into projects that speak to their hearts and souls. Investing in philanthropy, promotion of culture-wide diversity, inclusion training and awareness, and building humanitarian organizations feeds more than the balance sheet. With each passing quarter, more successful women are refocusing the power they garnered earlier in their careers into areas that benefit the greater whole of humanity.

Within this lies the opportunity to accept that power is malleable and can take on many faces. For some the C-Suite will be the ideal fit for life. Others will claim all the power the world has to offer and carry it in a new direction. Their fulfillment being found in implementing multiple executions for true service. And that is just the beginning of the story. As women claim their right to redefine power and leadership, amazing new presentations not yet dreamt are certain to emerge.

The Comfort Zone vs The Stretch Zone

Numerous psychological studies have revealed that a reluctant leader is typically possessed of sincere confidence in their abilities, while being unwilling to act or be seen as dogmatic or autocratic. The upswing is their propensity to give everyone a voice. They are the definition of inclusiveness. These are the leaders most naturally inclined to mentor promising team members in building their own equity. On occasion a reluctant leader faced with time restraints may feel pushed to take an authoritative stance. It is not unusual to find themselves surprised at the enthusiasm with which it is received by their team. These moments afford them the opportunity to understand where the fine line between inclusiveness and the team feeling untethered, rests. For the true leader, these lessons will be quickly absorbed, and new approaches implemented.

The fact that women are more empathetic than men has been extensively documented by scientific research. We've all heard the admonition, "do not mistake my kindness for weakness." This dilemma is one with which women have repeatedly wrestled. Some will lean too far into modeling a patriarchal, authoritarian approach. The greater majority can find themselves minimized due to their inherently inclusive sensibilities. Natural empathy grants women a deeper understanding of their team members which engenders greater loyalty. That commitment overflows from the leader to positively impact both a project and the company. This empathetic approach imbues team members with a feeling that they are an integral part of something versus just minions to be delegated to. Simultaneous to empowering them, it builds a commitment to the leader from which the entire organization benefits. Women's inclination toward inclusiveness and equity sharing often compels peers to seek their counsel. News spreads quickly that this individual gives her whole attention to listening and understanding. If someone is only looking for a sounding board, these women can assess this quickly and respond accordingly. If a peer finds themselves in sincere need of wise counsel, this is the person most likely to give their dilemma honest consideration before responding.

You will not find a woman who raises emotionally healthy kids, has a stable and vibrant partnership, elders who know they are well looked after, while successfully filling a leadership role, who has not mastered resilience. It touches everything she does. This is particularly visible in the leader who is passionate about her career. The reluctant leader is not a personality type who will settle for less. They express pride in everything they do, from their personal life to their professional commitments. From a broad stroke perspective, it's no state secret that women are their own most demanding accountability trackers. One aspect of accountability common within the reluctant leader is the ability to speak up and take responsibility. This is not someone who will deflect if the team is underperforming in accordance with the senior's expectations. When a single team member is out of line, the first place a reluctant female leader will look is to herself. Were the parameters clearly expressed? Was the team member placed on a project beyond their scope? Following a thorough assessment, effective action will be taken.

The vast number of things for which women are unfairly asked to take responsibility, has developed a strength in them that can serve well in the professional arena. Due to their unwillingness to lead themselves, the team, or the company astray, reluctant leaders stand above most others in the pursuit of life-long learning. You can recognize a reluctant leader through the way they are driven by the passion of their own magnetic north. While they will provide extraordinary service to the company, it is their joint allegiance to their own potential and passion that propels and drives them toward excellence. Above all else, the premier strength of a reluctant leader is she doesn't covet the position or its associate power. However, having accepted the mantle she will put the best of herself into fair administration of the role.

Business Talents Unique to Women

The axiom "it's not what you know, but who you know," is as old as business itself. While networking gatherings have traditionally been a means to this end, few professional women I've encountered enjoy this approach to business building and even fewer do it effectively. Their preferred venues are social events for professionals where networking feels like a natural extension of the conversation, rather than the conversation itself. Rachel Thomas, president of LeanIn.org says,

> *"I think men are socialized from the get-go to understand that mixing business and friendship is what you do to get ahead. We, as women, aren't as comfortable with doing that."*

Women are more likely to consider how they can benefit the other person before asking for something. Conversely, men are perfectly comfortable trusting the balance sheet will equalize over time. Additionally, due to the demands on them as primary caregivers within the family, attending after work or evening events can be difficult for women. They will factor in their traditional roles within the family, and the reality of often being the glue that holds everything together. This informs the necessity that their networking be both organic and nurture based. Women are more inclined to develop friendships and seek out other females with whom they can build long-term alliances. All of this begs the question of how women can best expand their sphere of influence. The most effective approach is to do what comes naturally. For that lesser percentage who enjoy networking and have mastered its nuance, don't fix what isn't broken. However, they might even consider adding to their repertoire of outreach vehicles.

Women who aren't comfortable in old-school networking meetings are best served by learning to maximize all the other gatherings they attend. Check out the networking events of any women's business groups to which you hold membership. You may discover some new approaches being implemented. If not, you may at least meet one new colleague. Instead of seeking out prospects, change the language. Identify new alliance partners. We all know a single personal introduction is worth hundreds of random business cards.

What Two People Do You Know That I Should Know

My very best tip came from an older friend who owned several sizable businesses and holdings in an unrevealed number of others. He was generous, nurturing, brilliant and a lifelong student. These traits had generated an extensive network of fans and collaborators that circled the planet. Over one of our monthly breakfast meetings I asked what he considered the most significant secret to his success. He responded that he never discussed any of his business interests with a new acquaintance. Neither did he bring them up at either official or casual networking events, even with people he already knew. Instead, he would ask everyone he met the same question. *"What 2 people do you know that I should know?"* For those he'd met previously and already asked his signature question, he changed it to, *"Who have you met in the past (6, 8, 10) months that I should know?"*

He explained that the 'ask' was always for 2 people, because being specific helped the other person's brain focus and present a clear answer. Over the years he had learned that by using a small number, those open to sharing rarely stopped with 2, and many offered to facilitate personal introductions. As was his way, he went on to say, *"The teaching moment* [in this conversation] *is never pitch or try to sell someone on you or what you represent. Respecting people enough to acknowledge that they have something more valuable than a mere purchase causes them to trip all over themselves to help you out. That level of respect disappeared from most business introductions a long time ago. That's the real power in the question."*

Another thing I can tell you of this man, from my own experience, is that he always respected the Law of Reciprocity. I once directed someone his way on the hunch they might be of benefit to one another. Despite nothing coming from that meeting, he still sent a thank you email. The second email I received that day was an introduction to one of his associates.

I started employing his question immediately, and the results have been unfailingly amazing. I have never lacked for contacts or clients. More significantly, many of the people to whom I posed this question upon our first meeting are still colleagues and collaborators many years after the fact.

The Self-Trust to Ask Our Value

While a growing number of top tier female leaders now have stay-at-home husbands, all-too-many who do not hold positions of that stature, still struggle to ask for salaries equal to their value. Thus, they also struggle to balance the financial strains associated with their greater lives. A recent conversation with a colleague who's spent years with one of NYC's top executive recruiting firms served as a poignant reminder of this. She was distressed about her experiences with the vast majority of women she works with, who are over 40. She shared her frustrations with how they consistently submit lower salary requests than the men who are seeking an equal role. Even when this colleague candidly tells a woman that she would be an ideal fit and that the company in question is highly motivated to balance the female, male representation within their executive suite, most of these same women will still not increase their salary requirements. They simply lack the self-confidence, the self-trust, to request a salary equal to their value.

While there is no denying that a deficit of self-trust is impacting both sexes, it is not spoken of directly in most business or personal development books. However, its symptoms certainly are. A few of the side effects with which we are most familiar are defensiveness, anxiety, worry, procrastination, hesitancy and self-doubt. And let's not overlook externalized gaps in our trust. Numerous studies conducted by the likes of Harvard, Johns Hopkins, UCLA Medical Center and The Brain Institute, to mention just a few, indicate that a lack of trust in another person, group, culture, or even situational examples of non-trust are all rooted in a lack of self-trust. Cultivating unwavering self-trust is an essential key for unlocking the doors previously closed to women. It is also a prerequisite to women collectively supporting one another. We cannot trust our female colleagues without first trusting ourselves. The internal questions of trust will cause us to constantly look for hidden motivations and agendas in others. Additionally, developing trust is vital in being able to leave a bigger world, full of limitless opportunities to our daughters and granddaughters. It will also equip us to model the benefits that gender parity produces to our sons.

So, let's jump into the heart or maybe I should say the mind of the matter. Studies in brain science reveal that over 90% of what we do on any given day is an emotional repeat of the past. Simply put, this means that even though we do different things and interact with different people, we are being driven by the same emotional framework, 90% of the time. In case that leaves you wondering, 'what!?!' Let me simplify. Consider how easy it is to resurrect the emotional turmoil of a past loss or upset. Or remember how easily specific *types* of situations can trigger past feelings of fear or pain. The old sensory reactions and mind-tapes created in those earlier moments have been activated and rush forward to dominate our attention. On the other hand, the full range of sensations from our happy events are not as readily accessible. We can recall them within our minds, but the full emotional impact is elusive. Each time the old emotions from past upsets rise to the surface, the same old fight, flight or freeze reaction is ignited. At the same time all the crippling self-perceptions that were born in those long-ago moments are activated as strongly as if it were a brand-new experience. This spontaneous revisiting of emotions imprinted in the past is a physiological event, originating in our limbic system. The limbic system learns through imprinting and repetition and speaks to us through the emotion of memory. Consequently, it governs habitual behaviors and mindsets, including all the earlier listed symptoms that point to a lack of self-trust.

Viewing another part of the brain, reasoning, learning, and creativity are primarily the dominion of our frontal lobes. This area aligns our focus and allows us to self-monitor, thereby giving us impulse control. This is the part of the brain that allows us access to our cognitive skills. It is critical in planning a successful future outcome and accessing our best self. The good news is that intentionally activating our frontal lobes lets our overtaxed limbic system settle a bit. Doing this as a pathway to self-trust is not hard. It simply requires consistency.

Let me be clear. I do not claim any level of accreditation or expertise in brain science. I offer this as an insight to what studying neuroscience allowed me to understand about my own positive and negative responses to life's events. It has been a powerful support in understanding the limiting mindsets behind my own expressions of resistance. Following that, it taught me how to reset my limiting thought processes and habitual behaviors.

Morning and Evening

The two most crucial parts of everyday life are how we begin it and how we end it. I'm going to share my best practices with you for both. These are processes that have not only proven effective in my own calming and settling, but have also served a large number of clients.

Morning

Starting the morning with mirror work sets you up to experience more self-confidence rooted in self-trust that helps you maintain a settled mindspace throughout your day.

Waking your frontal lobe up with self-trust sets a powerful foundation for your day. The first thing we all do when we get out of bed each morning is go to the bathroom. Instead of next stumbling immediately toward the coffee maker, pause.

Set a timer for 2 minutes:

Look into the mirror, directly into your eyes and say, "I love trusting me."

Avoid getting distracted by your morning hair.

Do not let your focus stray to that annoying imperfection you imagine yourself to have.

Also, don't start planning the details of your 10:00 meeting.

Give yourself permission to remain consciously present with yourself for two full minutes.

Extremely important is remembering that expressing trust for yourself doesn't begin and end with robotically delivered words. Intentionally feel the sensations of that trust moving through your body.

If you initially experience irritation or a desire to stop and mop the floor instead of continuing with your trust statement, *Congratulations*. This is a signal from your body. You are successfully connecting with the levels of yourself that are actively uncomfortable with self-trust. Gently and consistently repeat the statement. As the days pass it will become easier. Maintaining an intention to notice the occasions when you experience more self-trust during your daily interactions is helpful in recognizing your progress.

As acclaimed women's empowerment coach Natalia Benson explains in reference to self-acknowledgement practices,

"You'll notice it's easier to have tough conversations, like asking for a raise, firing someone, asking someone on a date, etc., because you're no longer avoiding yourself...."

Evening

It is broadly understood that what we take into our awareness just before sleeping will act to either settle or agitate our subconscious mind during our rest period. We've all had the experience of watching television or a movie and when we wake up the next morning, it's still playing in our mind. The reality is, that movie was rolling all night. This is why scientists recommend starting pre-sleep preparations at least 30 minutes before going to bed.

A recent article in Entrepreneur Magazine shared the following:

"Do a quick audit of the day. Acknowledging what went well each day keeps you from dwelling on what went wrong. Taking a moment to see the good in each day also helps you appreciate the progress you are making. Think of this as an exercise in gratitude, to remind yourself to be thankful for all you have."

For years I've had clients practicing a specific nighttime ritual to calm the mind and body in preparation for a restful sleep. It soothes the subconscious by giving it a gentle positive infusion before resting. This maximizes the restorative levels of sleep, while rewiring your mindset for self-trust. It's what I named *Victory Journaling* and could not be a simpler practice.

Start by purchasing a beautiful journal. Something truly pleasing to your eyes and that feels luxurious to touch. This is going to house all your amazing moments of great accomplishment, and a spiral notebook is simply not good enough for such valuable treasures.

Each evening when you crawl into bed and nestle under your comfy covers, open your Victory Journal and briefly outline a minimum of five things that you did exceptionally well that day. This can be anything from baking the best biscuits you've ever tasted in your life, to closing that big contract you spent months nurturing.

It doesn't matter what you write. It only matters that you choose to do it.

With each entry take a couple moments to feel the sensations of satisfaction for your accomplishment pulsing through your body.

For many women this will be the first time all day they stopped to give themself a dose of much-deserved self-appreciation. It's all-to-common for us to dash forward to the next thing after a success, instead of taking even a single personal moment. Victory Journaling is an act of giving ourselves permission to revel in a bit of self-appreciation.

Doing this every night is vital. Which will get you in better physical shape? Going to the gym and working out for four hours once a week or going to work out one hour every other day? Starting each morning by speaking love and trust to yourself followed by writing celebrations of your victories at bedtime creates a continuing cycle of expanded self-trust. Taking the extra moment to feel each personal acknowledgement adds rocket fuel to your self-trust development.

The degree of trust we feel for ourselves dictates our internal ease, therein our level of success in every area of life. It was inherent at birth. It fueled our courage to stand up for the first time and continue to try again each time we fell back on our diapers. Self-trust let us speed our bicycles down the road with wild abandon. Since that more innocent time, we've each known moments in life that have taken their toll on our trust, simultaneously muting our courage. The schoolyard kids that taunted and teased. The moments when, while usually well meaning, our mothers and fathers didn't possess the best parenting skills. The first lost job or the repeated rejections for a position. While, out of necessity we picked ourselves up and carried on, many of these experiences left pock marks in our self-trust. Those dents produced unhealthy habitual behavior patterns that fueled less than ideal mindsets.

I spoke of us rising to be our best selves and live our best lives. Don't rush yourself to get there or get discouraged when it takes a minute. This is a journey, not a destination. It doesn't matter where on the scale your self-trust currently rests. Consciously nurturing this aspect of yourself will reveal the strength, wisdom, tenacity, and potential that has been hidden away. Consistency is the key to a fulfilled life, and mastering self-trust is a necessary condition for establishing this. As the great writer and philosopher Ralph Waldo Emerson stated, *"Self-Trust is the essence of Heroism."*

Chapter Nine

"Like life, peace begins with women. We are the first to forge lines of alliance and collaboration across conflict divides."

~ *Zainab Salbi, author, founder and former CEO of Washington-based Women for Women International*

CEASE FIRE

I have worked with and been mentored by a number of savvy and supportive men, some who readily call themselves feminists. However, I am among the growing number of women who prefer to work predominantly with females. Wisdom seeded by my paternal grandmother delivered in her usual no nonsense tone when I was still a fledgling counseled, *"If you want something done well, ask the busiest woman you know."* As with all the golden nuggets she bestowed upon me this was held close to my heart and was well activated within my awareness. Personal experience has demonstrated that women often know how to succeed in great undertakings and are typically more fluid communicators. Time and again this has proven true within my professional, personal and social justice collaborations.

Now I readily admit this does not describe all women and I've certainly spent my fair share of time on the wrong end of that dynamic. Ironically, it was those experiences that refined my awareness around why it is imperative for women to establish inclusive alliances. All of the more tedious situations revealed a loss of both productivity and revenue. Then there was the damage to self-esteem and confidence. Each of these roadblocks belabored progression toward the designated goal. The cultures became toxic with competition, which stifled creativity and derailed problem-solving efforts. All expressions of woman-to-woman incivility weaken us as a whole. Building divides and cementing fears of working with women at all, comes at a severe cost to the pursuit of women's equity. Those from all sides of the equation lose, rendering adversity upon our greater society.

I speak with women weekly, who are gun-shy of working with other women due to past female-inflicted trauma. One of the commonly expressed dialogues is delivered by females who actively condemn women with all the stereotypical criticisms we've each heard before. These women will expose their internalized misogyny through a steadfast commitment to work exclusively with men, whenever possible. Only when professional circumstances force them to do otherwise will they tolerate the presence of a woman on the team. I'd be surprised to learn they do this with any enthusiasm or engaged support. Women aggressively condemning women alienates us from each other. The refusal to collaborate actively marginalizes the whole of us. Whether a woman chooses the path of excluding or actively denouncing other women is irrelevant. In every case, women's struggle to establish and expand their individual and collective equity is compromised.

A notable stimuli for mindsets that provoke women to oppress other women can be what psychologist's refer to as unevolved instinctual behavior. This is imprinting within our DNA from early historical periods. Throughout ancient times females were traditionally pitted against one another in physical combat. Tribal women of childbearing age were forced to compete for the strongest male. This was their sole means of achieving the status necessary to claim a lion's share of the meat from the hunts. Winners were regularly awarded first pick of the hides for clothing and blankets. The most coveted prize was an umbrella of protection from the tribe's alpha male, at least for the period of time that she could secure his favor. Having proven the necessary strength and will, the victor was awarded the honor(?) of birthing the strongest male's children. A female unable to produce offspring was shunned. Sent into the wilds to fend for herself, these women's lives were generally cut short. When one did carry to term, all credit for that child was bestowed upon the male and his paternal lineage. Children sired by the tribe's dominant warrior, specifically male babies, were deemed superior in every way. These orchestrated

144

competitions between women were believed to be as crucial to the health and preservation of the community as were power battles between the males. Successful propagation of a healthy next generation was prized second only to superior hunting skills for the tribe's continuation.

From our current state of evolution, these physical combats seem absurd. Nevertheless, the imprinting carried forward through our DNA can still be triggered. Environments dominated by unhealthy competition for status or what can even feel like personal survival, are prime catalysts. We can't rearrange our DNA, or instinctive impulses. We can stop, take a breath, and consciously choose our words along with the actions that follow. While understanding this ancient imprinting helps explain why we sometimes act as we do, remembering that we are not slaves to it, is freeing. Evolution has also provided us with the mental and emotional prowess to make rational, intentional choices. We can choose whether to continue actively alienating each other, or to listen, exhibit compassion, strive for understanding and elevate each other.

I believe that *women are each other's answer*. What my paternal grandmother accomplished in the early 1940's in cooperative partnership with another woman, left me with an unshakable confidence in the power of women's alliance. But, for women to collectively rise and claim the equity we deserve, we must stop waging war against each other. This includes ceasing to entertain the patriarchal programming that is rooted in competition and has dominated our culture for eons.

Patriarchy

Time and again I've heard female colleagues and acquaintances say, *"I just find men easier to get along with"*. This sentiment has been shared in professional environments, social settings, from female clients and even in spheres of social justice, more times than I can track. I've heard it as a justification for women declining an invitation to be a guest on my podcast, which focuses on women uplifting women. It has been a primary point of discussion at dinner parties, Friday night happy hours, and within female-based mastermind groups. I can't remember how long ago I was exposed to this fear-based attitude of exclusion and alienation. It seems to have always been there, and each time my heart breaks just a bit, for the woman speaking. She clearly doesn't realize all she forfeits by dissociating from those whose experience with oppression mirrors her own, simply because they too are female.

Traditional patriarchal thinking is another substantial contributor to why women alienate other women. Sociologists worldwide have published studies revealing that certain women will intentionally align with men due to the perception of them holding more power. This is leverage from which these same women hope to benefit by association, but it never works that way. Instead, all women are diminished.

Despite being most easily identified within the workplace, patriarchally minded women operate under the same standards in all arenas of life. We've each witnessed this. The socialite who achieves status via her husband's wealth and reputation. Women who gain seats on organizational boards due to their long and illustrious paternal heritage, each previous generation having been treasured patrons. Even the neighborhood bully can fall under this identification. The woman who works tirelessly to ensure everything, in what she deems her extended domain, is tucked in and properly regulated-in accordance with her clearly defined standards.

While discussing patriarchy, let's remember that it's not a reference to men, either generally or as a collective. Patriarchy is defined as, *"a system of society or government in which men hold the power and women are largely excluded from it"*. Through this definition we see that what sustains patriarchy is the system that has been perpetuated. While it was originally designed by and for men and they have been the long-term beneficiaries, a growing number of them are boldly championing feminist principles. Having to be the one and only, the sole player or top dog in every environment has been a burden that has taken its toll. It has been recognized that men have a shorter life-expectancy. They also suffer more heart-attacks, both fatal and those that are survived, but leave lingering consequences. Large numbers of men report a profound sense of emotional loss in respect to family connection and the heartache of having missed out on so many of their children's more significant milestones.

Women wielding patriarchal mindsets are typically steadfast in their commitment. Unfortunately, this is sans the conscious recognition of the internalized misogyny that has possessed their minds, lives, and actions. They assume their perceptions are resolutely correct, in the sense of all else being incorrect or at the very least, inadequate. This internalized misogyny can make them the strongest enforcers of patriarchal standards of behavior. The girls and young women over whom they hold authority are often emotionally traumatized anytime they dare to display their uniqueness. Women driven by internalized misogyny remain vigilant to indoctrinating both our young females and males. Their children or grandchildren are regularly unbraided with, "girls don't", "young women shouldn't", "you're too loud", "too bossy", "too outspoken", "boys don't like girls who _____", "they don't want a girl that would or doesn't _____", and the diatribes continue. The young girls and boys are both programmed with a mindset that requires the girls to always be the ones who conform, while the boys are expected to run free and be a bit wild. When boys and girls become more physically close or intimate than what is generally acceptable, the fault is irresolutely placed on the girl.

It's a time-old saga of robbing females of their individual personhood from the time they can walk and talk. This rigid patriarchal training compels girls and young women to relentlessly search for external acceptance. They work tirelessly to shape themselves into boxes created by anyone around them. The struggle to feel worthy of receiving the love and encouragement to which they are inherently entitled invariably finds them feeling without and often lost. This carries through their school years, girls belittling, judging, ostracizing other girls. Who is cute, who is not? Who is too free with her burgeoning sexuality? Who is too rigid? The impact of these harsh expectations and perpetual judgments often cripple a girl's self-image. A burden that carries into adulthood and is passed onto their daughters is another and more recent demonstration of unevolved instinctual behavior. The patriarchy and its associate, internalized misogyny, live to impair a new generation.

There will continue to be those women who shun other women as a means of maintaining their patriarchal thinking and internalized misogyny. However, there are many more who do not fit this mold. I regularly speak with those who long to encounter other women with whom they can collaborate in the creativity and compassion that is natural to the female gender. Often their explanation for not pursuing these relationships is the fear of being on the receiving end of woman-to-woman incivility, again. So how do we heal the scars of our youth, move beyond the fear of harm at the hands of other women and build successful alliances?

Like all things relational, the strength of any alliance will be dictated by the comfort we have established in our own skin. As greater numbers of women begin practicing unapologetic self-appreciation, this will heal the old wounds and fuel a new vibrancy for life.

What is Our Best Self

We've all heard the words 'be your best self'. They sound good. But how many of us devote consistent attention to learning how that feels, what it looks like, what speaking from our best self sounds like? Living from our best self is an internal invitation to adventure beyond the limitations of the fears we've held fast and the wounds we've worked to protect at all costs. It requires that we view ourselves with fierce candor. It demands we set down the habit of external comparison which alternately triggers either competition or defeatism. In short, we must venture beyond the restrictive parameters of our comfort zones. Stepping up to experience new things is a daring move, particularly if a similar step did not turn out well in the past. Discovering our best self requires nurturing the courage to boldly venture into unknown territory with no promise that it will turn out as we intend.

One of the more powerful expressions our best self demonstrates is generosity. This is typically thought of as an external offering to others and that's a large part of the problem. Learning to be generous with ourselves is a completely new experience for a majority of women. It is our best self that endows us with the largesse of spirit that lets us laugh at our own mistakes. Viewing our mis-steps with humor or the curiosity to learn something new leaves little room for others to use them against us. This finer level of who we are leads us to the freedom available in competing with no one but ourselves. Doing so from self-directed kindness and wisdom opens our minds and hearts to simultaneously appreciate other's gifts and talents.

Our best self is who we are at our core. From this level we discover the deepest purpose for our being here on the planet. Courage, kindness, inclusivity, and curiosity are just a few of the soul nurturing traits our best selves possess. Becoming this aspect of ourselves infuses us with a passion for life itself. This is the spark that lights up as we envision ourselves as capable of fulfilling our greatest dreams. It is the energy that lights up the room as we sit with someone, hearing their heart and letting them know they are truly being heard. Under the exhilarating influence of our best self we are able to fall in love with everything that life has to offer. Enthusiastically celebrating every little success becomes natural.

Unlike our worry centered mind, our best self does not mislead us into fruitless searches for perfection. It helps us recognize this as nothing more than an illusion. Perfectionism is clarified as a non-existent state. Setting down this exhausting cultural addiction allows us the psychic and emotional space to revel in being simply present. When we live as our best self, we can decide that giving our best and doing our best is enough. There is deep relief available in becoming satisfied with the moments of simply being enough. Becoming our best selves is a direct path to accepting our fundamental worthiness. The anxiety caused by competition dissolves along with all the other symptoms of perfection seeking.

So, that all sounds good but how do we get there? First remember this is a marathon, not a sprint. As with anything developed for sustainability starting with small, consistent steps will produce the most far-reaching results. Building a new and more honest affinity for ourselves requires the same energy as developing an external relationship. We listen, communicate, and offer care, but this time, from the inside out. Unleashing our best selves to guide us through life makes us the primary beneficiary of all it has to offer. Befriending this self and listening to its inner messages also helps us notice the areas where we've already seeded self-appreciation. These small recognitions grant us the confidence to gently progress toward bigger and bolder steps.

We've all heard the saying, *know your weaknesses*. Positivity is the energy on which our best self-thrives. It understands we don't have weaknesses, per se, only areas in which we are not as skilled, practiced or strong. Most significantly, our best self loves us beyond measure. It is the quiet, gentle voice reminding us to not overextend our bodies, minds or other resources. This level of our being delights in showing us ways to honor our personal bandwidth, mentally, emotionally, physically, energetically and psychically.

A big part of getting to know this kinder, more giving inner level is paying attention to when we are suppressing it. This is an easy step. Notice when you fall back into the time old struggle to become enough. Taking a timeout to review all the personal assets you have already fine tuned helps to refocus your attention and subsequently your actions. Anytime you feel insufficient or unprepared, you've fallen back into the sandpit. While you may not be perfect, you are likely closer to your goal than your fears would have you imagine. The mere fact that you don't feel prepared is a message that you do have some concept of what prepared will feel like. Take a walk, even for five minutes. Don't think about what's troubling you. Give your mind and energy a short break and return fresh. Dive back in as if it were a new day with a clean blank canvas.

Perfection chasing comes naturally to humans and particularly to women. The majority of us were taught from girlhood that we were a bundle of flaws and failings that require constant work to remain concealed. Our best self knows that this exists only in our habitual mind. The current moment is always the best time to stop playing this wicked game against yourself. It's a brutal internal competition with no potential winner.

Only in shifting away from these merciless traditions do we start to breathe with our whole lungs, feed our cells and discover the fun available in life. For years I was a queen of leveraging these dehumanizing thought patterns upon myself. Even after recognizing them for what they were, I wasn't sure of how to break them, or if it was even possible. The decades I spent torturing myself with comparison against everyone and everything left a seemingly unfillable hole in my gut. My mind running in endless circles as if trapped in a race I was constantly losing. All those years of riding the radar's fine line were a result of my internal conviction that I wasn't smart enough, thin enough, wealthy enough, or just enough. In my mind I was fundamentally less than virtually everyone around me. The symptoms of competition, comparison and perfection seeking were clear but unidentified as such.

The other thing that remained constant was my desire to break free. I relentlessly chased studies in psychology, brain science, personal development and any other thing that crossed my way. Little by little, one step at a time the intensity of the shame over my unending list of flaws began to lessen. No longer living the life of a proverbial gypsy, I'd stopped running but I was still plagued by the feeling of being insufficient. During one morning meditation the words rang through my mind as clear as a bell. *"Perfection is overrated. Just go out and be awesome."* While the words made immediate sense they didn't slow my perfection chasing, and the message didn't fade either. It was as if it had created an instant brain loop that would sporadically start playing at any random moment of the day.

Slowly, over the period of a couple months I realized that without missing a beat I'd tricked myself into changing the rules of the game. Instead of comparing and competing with everyone else I was comparing myself against what free might mean, what *enough* could potentially feel like. The quest to arrive at some ever-serene place had become a competition against where I was at any given moment. Each fluctuation in my hard-fought self-image was a sign of failure. I wasn't *perfectly* self-confident. The anxiety wasn't *perfectly* banished. My sense of freedom wasn't *perfectly* intact. All followed by the criticism that if I would just stop perfection chasing what I would discover in myself would be enough. Finally, one day I collapsed on the couch having completely exhausted myself with it all. A moment later clarity came like a slideshow running through my mind. I'd done such a brilliant job of trying to escape my not enoughness by locking myself into perfection chasing that I'd made it impossible to set down. So, I'd simply pointed the old habit in a new, but equally punishing, direction. Somehow the absolute absurdity of it all struck me as hilarious. After this, every time the old cycle would reemerge, and it did, I would take myself back to that moment of preposterous realization. It wasn't always the soothing balm it had been that first time but it did remind me that this too will pass. And, it always does.

Consider marking or tagging this page. On days that feel too-much, not-enough, or out of sync, reflect back to see where you might be muting the voice of your best self. Take a few moments to sit in silence or settle into a nurturing bath. Notice where you are competing. Is this competition an externalized exercise or an internal punishment? Feel where your body is tight with the restriction that comes from chasing perfection. Mentally and emotionally revisit any moment when the ease of being your best self was filling your day. You'll find yourself relaxing into a more self-appreciative heartspace. After all, your best self didn't go anywhere. You simply got distracted from its influence and wandered into old and familiar patterns. These days will turn up and when they do, be gentle with yourself

Learning how it feels to walk through life as your best self does not mean you'll never have another anxious moment or hard day. It simply means you no longer need to stretch it out into several weeks and continue to feel lost with no help in sight. You now have a road map with directional indicators to resettle into a comfortable space within your own skin. Resting into your best self can dissolve the fears of approaching other women as collaborators. Your potential for developing creative alliances has exponentially amplified.

Getting Real with Ourselves

Getting real with ourselves around how we feel about other women is our most productive next step. Discovering *why* we leap to judgment will tell us far more about ourselves than them.

Over the years the following questions have served a number of female clients to realize their gender-based biases.

This is not a 1-10 scale through which you're invited to turn the judgment around on yourself, rather an opportunity for fierce self-honesty. Take a few minutes with each to feel deeply into your most transparent truth.

1. How quickly do you lean into judging other women for making choices you imagine yourself never making?

2. What is your internal response to women less savvy than you imagine yourself?

3. Do you look for flaws that will let you criticize women who have accomplished more than you?

4. How likely are you to reach out in support of a younger female colleague who is stumbling on a particular project?

5. When a new female joins the team, are you immediately welcoming or do you feel the need to first sit back and scrutinize?

6. Do you prefer to work with women? Men? No preference? Why?

7. Do you prefer to work for women? Men? No preference? Why?

8. Would you prefer to join a collaborative project with a woman? Man? No preference? Why?

9. When attending a professionally focused social event, do you first gravitate to the senior females or males? Why is this choice more comfortable? Is it a choice or a habit?

10. When seeking new or specialized mentoring, do you seek out a female? Male? It doesn't matter?

What is the relevance of the questions comparing one's reaction to women vs men, you quite possibly wondered? Regardless of what triggers judgment, the greater percentage of the sum total typically falls into the area of 'passive'. Criticisms, censures, and negative assessments can become so habitual that we easily look past them, what they are and how they dictate our interactions. Becoming uncompromisingly honest with ourselves requires examining our most deeply hidden secrets, especially those withheld from ourselves. Discovering any unconscious bias creates more space for the inclusivity required to build alliances. Consequently, clearing those hidden corners naturally gives us access to the voice and impulses of our best self. It fuels our inner strength, therein granting us expanded personal ease which extends to those around us. Potentially the most significant benefit of fierce self-honesty is that every avenue to self-acceptance gives us a greater sense of personal freedom. Whether we are focusing on our strengths or fragilities this remains always true.

Building Alliances

As women we've all been in the same sociologically, psychologically, professionally marginalized position since time immemorial. While we have not each dealt with it in the same way, the stigmas and imposed limitations exist for all of us. From this vantage point it becomes clear that we have ever-so-much in common. Can we cease actively alienating each other long enough to recognize this? Accepting that we are not inherently each other's nemesis frees our mental, emotional, and psychic space to accept that there is enough room, money, professional real-estate, and even desirable partners for all of us.

At the 2009 Vancouver Peace Summit, the Dalai Lama famously said, *"The world will be saved by the western woman"*. What is less known is that he prefaced this statement with, *"some people may call me a feminist."* This begs the question, why would the Dalai Lama being feminist be a bad thing? But to live out his prediction it will be necessary to allow our best selves to rise and to lead.

My own collaborative alliances with women have secured my resolute belief that personal and global levels of both equity and equality are attainable. But this can only happen as a great wave of women adopt intentional inclusivity. My most heartfelt invitation when speaking to groups of women is, *"Cultivate the curiosity of what can I contribute"*. Continuing in the tired old tradition of what can I get, will get us just what we got, feeling alone with fewer resources than we deserve. Collectively, we do possess the power to be each other's answer when we join in alliance and actualize the brilliant potential that's just itching to rise within each of us.

To foster inclusivity let's start by remembering that alliance building is innate to most women. Studies have revealed that women naturally lean more strongly into building alliances vs establishing networks. Based on extensive research for her bestseller, *"The Healing Power of Girlfriends: How to Create Your Best Life Through Female Connection"*, Deborah A. Olson states,

> *"Women thrive on connection, and research studies continue to show that we are happier and healthier when we share close connections with other women."*

So, where do we start when building intentional alliances with women? Begin identifying the value you could reap by participating within a circle of creative females. A good launch point for this is to consider what type of alliances are currently most important to you. Where do you feel you're falling behind, not advancing as quickly as you'd like? In what areas do you feel you would benefit from fresh input? What new skills would you like to develop? Are there new directions of personal development you'd like to explore, and have mind-share alliances with whom to partner on this?

Create a chart for identification purposes and be specific about all your areas of focus. These simple tables will guide you in getting started.

See Table 7: Building Alliances - Professional on page 158

See Table 8: Building Alliances - Advocacy on page 159

See Table 9: Building Alliances - Other on page 159

If you find the next step to be challenging, know that you're in good company. Many women unfamiliar with reaching out confidently, initially find this awkward.

When encountering a woman from an area you have identified on your chart, take the necessary time to connect. If this is someone with a higher position or more influence, all the more reason. Rise to the challenge and step out of your comfort zone. Many women spend endless years crippling themselves with the fear of not revealing what they do not yet know. This is precisely the purpose of developing broad-based alliances. Additionally, building an expanded comfort zone is the fastest way to shatter the limitations of the old one. All alliance building is founded in a desire to both receive and extend support. This is a powerful pathway to discovering more of one's potential. The easiest way to accomplish this is to learn from those who have already walked the path. So, step up for yourself. Be audaciously bold, for just 60 seconds. Initiate that conversation and see what happens. She will be open to establishing a connection or she won't. Either way you'll have put a good dent in your self-constructed wall of limitation.

How many appointments, intended to expand your circle of influence, have you canceled at the last minute by claiming time restraints? The percentage of unpaid labor for which women have been trained to take total responsibility has been crippling to equity building through expanding alliances. Does the spontaneous reply, *"That would be great, but I don't have the time"* sound familiar? Becoming strongly aligned within an expanding circle of women who offer support, input, tips, encouragement and female camaraderie will require delegating. Just as completing all the requirements of our professional life demands the same.

Delegating in one's non-work life can be challenging for women. Many have never considered the possibility. A term I learned from a dear friend that I have since employed regularly is MWS, 'money well spent'. Many women can't justify the expense of having their homes cleaned weekly. However, having someone in to do the deep work once a month can free up an entire day, or two, for more fruitful engagements. How many time-consuming tasks that devour your hours and exhaust your energy, can you start delegating? Are the potential benefits of developing new female alliances worth employing a childcare professional for an hour every few weeks or once a month?

Another area where women trip themselves is trying to squeeze meetings that would benefit their professional lives into their personal hours. Maybe a proposed appointment isn't specific to what you are working on at this particular moment. Nevertheless, if a meeting with a potential new alliance partner today will support your professional life next month, schedule it during the workday. Professional men do this regularly, with no guilt, shame or remorse. It is a significant contributor to their success. The fact that women have not felt free to employ this tradition is a detriment to both their careers and personal lives. Take the opportunity to establish that strategic alliance without shortchanging your non-work hours.

Table 7: Building Alliances
PROFESSIONAL

PROFESSIONS	ALLIANCE GROUP POTENTIALS
What Industry ie Marketing, STEM, Finance, Economics, etc.	
Entrepreneurs ie Consultancy, Personal Mentoring, Diversity Implementation Consultants, etc.	
Business Owners ie Business Mgnt & Consultants, Eco-Respectful Consumer Products	
Speakers ie Resilience, Equity, Company Culture, Developing Excellence	
Leadership ie C-Suite, Agility, Developing Influence, Relationship Building	
Other ie Organization Builders, Influencers, Change Makers	

Table 8: Building Alliances
ADVOCACY

PROFESSIONS	ALLIANCE GROUP POTENTIALS
Social Justice ie Voting Rights, Climate Justice, Racial Injustice, Refugee Justice, Hunger & Food Insecurity, LGBTQIA	
Community Justice ie Family Group Conferencing, Neighborhood Conferencing, Law Enforcement and Citizen Relationship Restoration	
Community Organizer ie Non-Government Community Development, Community Organizing for Support of Kids	
Other ie Senior Support, Industry Specific Advocacy for Equality & Equity	

Table 9: Building Alliances
OTHER

PROFESSIONS	ALLIANCE GROUP POTENTIALS
Personal Development ie Time Management, Growth Mindset, Resiliency, Personal Presence	
Life / Work Balance ie Family, Health, Professional, Personal, Purpose	

159

Power Partners—Equity and Alliance

Well established relationships are indispensable in every area of life. They create a dependable foundation for alliance by building emotional equity. Attentive listening, exhibiting concern and showing empathy, places us in good stead with everyone we encounter. In fact, starting from the intention of establishing broad emotional equity, is the easiest way to find yourself surrounded with strategic alliance partners.

Emotional equity is a people-first approach. Being founded on 'team' and 'we' instead of the traditional 'me' and 'I' perspective. It's a natural fit for building alliances. Emotional equity is an every voice matters approach and is applicable in all areas of life.

So, how do we build equity in a manner that naturally expands our strategic alliance base? Review your answers to the charts on page 158 - 159 that outlined the areas relevant to your current life focus. Add the information from the following strategies to expand that same chart.

1. Make a list of all the women you currently know who are well established under each area on your list.

2. Add those women who are already equipped with the skills you identified as areas of your own interest.

3. Keep a running list of new women you meet. Make notes on what you learned about them as launch points for your next conversation.

4. Develop your own personal Board of Directors. (A tip Jane Bradley, from chapter 5, gave me some years ago.) Choose a diverse group of female advisors and collaborators. These will be women you can consult regarding your career, social justice projects, volunteerism, and anything else on your original list.

5. Reach out to connect with 2-3 women each month for a brief conversation. This can be in person or virtually.

6. Drop a 'brief' 2 to 3 sentence email after each call or meeting. Thank the woman for her time and cite what she shared that was of benefit.

7. Follow up on any commitments made in a timely manner.

8. Remember that the *Law of Reciprocity* is crucial to both building equity and developing alliances. Openly ask how you can bring value to any initiatives she is currently spearheading. If there is nothing in the moment, extend the invitation to feel welcome to connect at a future time. If you are aware of a project she is building and know someone who may be supportive, send an introductory email without waiting to be asked for a referral.

Reach out beyond your old borders. Give yourself permission to defy the limitations of your comfort zones. Be bold enough to discover new, supportive, female-based connections. Albeit an old axiom, the truth remains that *fortune favors the bold.*

The value of joining with a group of women to brain-share on any area of commonality cannot be overstated. Through time you will come to know one another's strengths and the areas where you each commonly trip. With these insights you are positioned to be each other's champions and cheerleaders. A sense of camaraderie develops along with an ease of flow when supporting each other in a specific area of advancement. This is the foundation of meaningful alliance.

Start by creating a small group of women who meet consistently, once a month. They don't have to be from the same company or even the same industry. Thanks to our exploding virtual world, they need not be from the same state. This type of group has proven deeply satisfying for myself and many others. I am gratefully involved in three different women's groups. One focuses on the challenges inherent to being a female entrepreneur. Another group focuses on uncovering our unconscious bias and furthering social justice initiatives. The third group combines entrepreneurs and founders of woman owned and operated businesses.

Groups specific to one area of life produce accelerated growth opportunities for all those actively involved. Sharing the experiences, challenges and resolutions of women from different histories, professions, cultures, and regionalities empowers all the group members. Additionally, receiving support, tips and insights from such groups, reminds every woman involved of the uniqueness we each bring to any table. Factoring in everything the average woman balances within her world, opportunities to be reminded of our value can register like life-sustaining oxygen.

Developing alliance groups can be particularly beneficial to women who have achieved senior leadership positions. Too often they are expected to dedicate great amounts of time to sharing from their wealth of knowledge, while finding themselves without similar support. Taking the lead in creating a small group of equals who can serve as sounding boards, encouragers, and idea vetting partners could produce a powerful foundation for previously absent mental, emotional reinforcement.

As we come together in greater numbers, we can create a power shift from the antiquated paradigms, to a new dynamic of inclusivity. However, this can only occur as we set down the true antagonist in this story, our long-taught fear of each other. From the vantage point of inclusivity, we position ourselves to create much needed, long-term solutions, for ourselves, our daughters and our communities.

Building Equity While Up-Leveling the Culture

In recent years the topic of company culture has taken center stage. A highly successful businessman whose work I've followed for years is fond of saying, *"The problem with companies these days is not a lack of culture. Every company has a culture. Unfortunately, too many of those are not intentionally created. This means too many company cultures are formed by the loudest voice, which is never the voice you want to have in power."*

The companies to which he refers are those in which pitifully few of the employees devoting their time, energy, and years of their life have an opportunity to build real equity. Equity tends to be viewed through a segmented and compartmentalized lens. We read articles and books discussing professional equity, emotional equity, social equity, academic equity, and so on. Emotional equity being a people-first approach makes it key to success in all arenas of equity development.

The following are valuable actions I help female clients execute to support other women. Implementation has shown that their own equity is simultaneously enhanced through demonstration of superior leadership skills.

Magnify the Skills and Assets Women Bring to the Table

- When a woman is interrupted during a meeting, tell her you'd like to hear the rest of her thought. You'll have empowered this woman to bring her big idea to the table without minimizing anyone else present.

- Publicly recognize women for the ideas and contributions they brought to a project. Allowing the team to witness your expression of respectful recognition illustrates ways for them to build their own equity. It encourages everyone to bring their best forward. The net result of this being a highly engaged workplace culture.

- When the proposals of a woman you know to be smart and consistently well prepared are dismissed out of hand, ask her to expand on the potential benefits. As women lead in giving more floor space to other women, a new tone of inclusivity, alliance and equity building is established.

Support Women Who Appear to be Stumbling

- Being available as an engaged source of support is a fast track to building equity within the team. Ask how you can help.

- Rather than telling a female team member how to approach a challenge, share a relatable story of how you succeeded in a similar circumstance. This approach promotes self-confidence by offering support while letting another discover her own specific solution.

- Offer to be a sounding board for another woman's ideas. Often hearing ourselves talk something through, will land us at a resolution point previously overlooked.

Speak Up When You Overhear Incivility Toward a Woman

- When this occurs, in separate and private conversations, allow both the woman being maligned and the offender to know you do not support such behavior within the workplace. The recipient of the incivility will appreciate knowing someone spoke up on her behalf. Concurrently, the offending party will become clear about your workplace boundaries. The confidentiality of the conversation allows them to be redirected without humiliation. This establishes equity with both.

- If you hold a superior role and overhear a woman being chastised in front of others, quietly invite the offender to your office for a conversation. Demonstrating the behaviors you expect from your team clearly defines cultural expectations within the workplace. Not only is your equity as a leader increased, but it is also a valuable lesson to team members in their own equity building efforts.

The core definition of equity is, *"the quality of being fair and impartial"* *"without cheating or trying to achieve unjust advantage"*. To gain a reputation equal to this assures us of continued access to ongoing support and respect. Even more importantly, it gives us the ability to feel secure in our own skin and sleep restfully.

Punch Above Your Weight Class

One of the common tripping points that holds women back is the fear of reaching up. They hesitate to approach women with more finely honed skills or who have achieved a status that they cannot yet imagine themselves possessing. What so many women fail to consider is that women of stature have long since overcome this barrier. Their current standing speaks directly to having been eager students to those who went before them.

Subsequently, many of these more accomplished women will enthusiastically share what they have learned, in the spirit of paying it forward. Without the generosity of my dear mentors who I introduced in chapter 5 much of what I've achieved may have lain dormant, untapped. We all enjoy being appreciated for our unique skills and talents. Attentively presented requests for support, insight or guidance is an expression of respect.

Muster the courage to place yourself in the rarified air space of the broadly accomplished. It is our most accessible path to gaining the knowledge that will reveal our most potent potential.

One thing I have long witnessed to be true of women is we are audacious. Mirriam Webster defines it as, *"having a willingness to take surprisingly bold risks"* as being, *"fearless, intrepid, adventurous, gutsy"* and yes, *"heroic"*. Imagine groups of women with each of these traits joining an alliance. As we cease to distance and compete, what *can't* we accomplish together?

Chapter Ten

"I've written eleven books but each time I think, 'Uh oh, they're going to find out now. I've run a game on everyone and they're going to find me out.'"

~ *Maya Angelou; author, poet, memorist,
playwright, civil rights activist*

IMPOSTER SYNDROME

I openly acknowledge I have done many things that few women I personally know have accomplished. Equally there are more women than I can count who have outdistanced me. I have more than a handful of friends who have spoken of my having lived a big life. Then there are the many women I look up to as seeming larger than life itself. It is the women whose triumphs I cannot imagine reaching for that I have always measured myself against. A crippling habit practiced by too many of us. The big story I made up that chased me with relentless fervor was that my own successes were virtually all due to having been the luckiest person I know. My other most common go-to dismissals of personal accreditation typically read, "oh, I've simply followed my nose." or, "every notable thing I've done just came to me." As if it walked right up and presented itself. Luck, stumbling along until I tripped over something significant, and being tracked down by good fortune. Those were the stories that let me continue to reach for the next higher rung. All the while I privately trembled at my imagined absence of qualification and the assurance I would one day be recognized as a phony. This meant I had to always keep running. Standing still long enough to internalize my victories might result in someone seeing through the thin veneer to spot my fraudulence.

Therefore, nothing prior to months of sitting in quiet focus to write this book had brought me so blatantly face to face with my sense of being an imposter. I'd been aware of *Imposter Syndrome* for years. Each analysis I studied provided a clear description of my own behaviors. Applying the newest techniques presented, the immediate roar would subside. But no amount of work on myself produced a permanent stay on the mental tapes decrying my credibility, until I happened upon something that demanded I acknowledge the distortions that were convincing me that I was a fraud.

Starting to write was easy. I had a passion swirling inside that was surging toward its own release. Knowing what I wanted to say was not an issue. I'm certainly not devoid of perspectives or informative research and its associated data. Crafting it into sentences that I found acceptable was another thing. Each new chapter found me staring at a blank page for days on end, certain that I had already spent all the words I possessed. Finishing it, facing the reality of being published, was arguably the hardest leg of the journey. If it flopped any lingering hope that my imposter status was just a self-diminishing fantasy would be dashed. If it didn't...I never fully identified what that would mean. Only the sense that I had bashed an internal hornet's nest with the biggest broom I could find and my imposter status was at risk of no longer remaining my own well-kept secret. So, I worked and reworked everything but the conclusion until it became an absurd exercise in delaying the inevitable. A classic *Imposter Syndrome* technique.

In 1978 Pauline Claunce and Suzanne Ines coined the term *"Imposter Syndrome"* to describe the female confidence challenge. *"Women frequently express that they don't feel they deserve their job and are "imposters" who could be found out at any moment."* As Claunce and Ines identified, this delusive self-perception affects a disproportionate number of women. What has since become understood is that its impact on women of color is even more crippling. *"We're more likely to experience imposter syndrome if we don't see examples of people who look like us or share our background who are clearly succeeding in our field,"* states clinical psychologist, Emily Hu. This makes perfect sense considering how many women wrestle for a sense of self-confident autonomy. Reality TV is just one of the more insidious vehicles for objectifying women. Most females represented as successful are portrayed by women who fit a narrow spectrum of physical appeal. An overwhelming percentage of them are the fair-complected, Euro stereotype. Those not fitting the celebrity esque complexion, body shape and fantasized image of femininity are covertly undermined. All women outside that narrow window of thin, white, Euro-descent physical presentation continue to suffer from lack of representation. Women of color are undeniably subjected to the most exaggerated displacement of positive self-imaging.

This false belief system of being frauds is not limited to those of us whose names never appear in business publications or newspapers. Neither are its effects only felt by women outside the idealized perceptions of what is desirable. Many women of great accomplishment have openly admitted to experiencing the gut-twisting effects of *Imposter Syndrome*. Among those are 3-time Oscar winner, 21-time Oscar nominee, actress Meryl Streep, playwright, actress, comedian, writer, and producer, Tina Fey, founder of Nasty Gal, Girlboss Media, and New York Times bestselling author, Sophia Amoruso, Facebook COO and founder of LeanIn.Org, Sheryl Sandberg, Shark Tank's Barbara Corcoran and even former First Lady Michelle Obama and Supreme Court Justice Sonia Sotomayor.

The majority of women, including those just listed, describe *Imposter Syndrome* as internal wrestling matches that rise in periodic episodes. Each is generally triggered by facing a big move, project or accomplishment. They are aware of the difference between the feelings of a general dip in self-confidence and the sensations of being an imposter. The very specific sense of being a fraud is all too familiar, therein easily identifiable.

Key Indicators of Imposter Syndrome

According to expert Dr. Valerie Young, author of *The Successful Thoughts of Successful Women*, there are five different ways people mistakenly view their own competence.

1. *"The Perfectionist: expects everything they do to be flawless. So, they feel shame if they fall short."*

2. *"The Superwoman: expects to excel not just in her work but in all of her multiple roles as parent, partner, community member, etc."*

3. *"The Natural Genius: believes the only true success is innate and effortless. So, if they have to struggle to master a skill or pass an examination, they assume they are a fraud."*

4. *"The Rugged Individualist: thinks the only achievements that count are those that are unassisted. So, their need to ask for help or tutoring would indicate ineptness."*

5. *"The Expert: feels they need to be highly credentialed – yet even when supremely qualified they fear they never know enough."*

Don't panic or wind up the self-criticizing tapes if more than one of these sounds familiar. Humans are complex and women even more so. It's quite common to exhibit several of the impostor characteristics. The upside being that within each exist multiple clues to help you identify how you are participating with *Imposter Syndrome*, and we do cooperate with the syndrome. Giving into its symptoms to the degree of offering them credence allows them power over our minds and actions. One of the most confusing symptomatic cycles it presents is alternating feelings of 'fear of success' and' fear of failure'.

This is exemplified by; Overworking to the point of physical, emotional, mental exhaustion to prove:

- How much [more] it takes for you to succeed.

- A potentially paralyzing fear of making mistakes, Thus proving you are a fraud. (According to the dictates of *Imposter Syndrome* every mistake qualifies as an overall failure.)

- Conversely, an unconscious dread of success you would gauge as significant. (It can place you in a spotlight which will expose your status as a fraud. Thus, derailing recognition of your overall success in life.)

Additional signals of *Imposter Syndrome* include:

- Anything that isn't perfect lacks real value. (Since perfection is an illusion, you are able to chronically minimize every accomplishment.)

- An inability to internalize compliments. ("Anyone could have done it." "It's just part of the job." "All in a day's work.")

- Successes are minimized or deflected. ("It was a team effort; I was just a participant." or "I was lucky. Everything fell together so easily.")

- Hyper-focus on things that did not rise to an unrealistic standard ("That was okay, but...if only I'd")

- Obsessing over small things that were left incomplete. ("How could I have missed that? It was so obvious!")

- Being a chronic overachiever. (This is the only way to be *barely* enough for one in the throes of *Imposter Syndrome*.)

- Incessantly feeling like a fraud, exacerbated by the fear that someday, you will be exposed and all will be lost. (This is one reason fewer women ask for promotions or salary increases. When they do ask for financial enhancements, it is generally more gently framed and for a lesser amount than what a male equal would *assertively lobby*.)

With any self-minimizing mindset that drives anxiety, slowing down to address it directly is the single means to overcoming it. The same is true with *Imposter Syndrome*. Acknowledging the core source allows you to successfully address the symptoms. Next, revealing the ways it is plaguing you with trusted confidants can start to ease the internal pressure. You may be surprised to discover that numerous female friends or colleagues relate to your experience. Realizing you are not alone often proves to be liberating.

Six additional tips for sidelining the consequences of Imposter Syndrome are:

1. Notice the internal signs. When you start to feel your mind cloud with imposter-speak, or notice you are procrastinating, take affirmative action, immediately.

2. Keep a log of your successes. This will serve as a touchstone when you feel yourself getting bogged down with 'imposter' mind-speak.

3. Develop a set of strategies for addressing mistakes. Henry Ford once said, *"Failure is only the opportunity to begin again more intelligently."* The focus is on 'more', not 'intelligently'. Within each mis-step exists a teaching moment. Focus on what you learned instead of what didn't go in the direction you intended. It will save you the need of repeating the course.

4. Shift the inner narrative. All *Imposter Syndrome* is based on wildly undocumented imaginings. When your tapes start rolling in the direction of, *"This is it. They're all going to see that I have no idea what I'm doing,"* remind yourself of something that is indisputably true. My favorite two fallbacks are, *"Serena Williams started playing professionally in 1995 and because she didn't quit, ultimately won her first Grand Slam in 1999. She is now arguably the greatest female tennis player in history."* Or, instead of thinking, *"Everyone else attending will be brilliant. I just can't do this. I'll feel like the dumbest person in the room"* Shift to, *"That room is going to be full of brilliant people. There is no way I'm going to miss out on all I'll learn from this experience."*

5. Visualize having fun learning and succeeding. Begin each day with 10-15 minutes of relaxing into a visualization. See and *feel* yourself being excited each time the unknown is thrown your way. See and *feel* yourself enjoying everything you are learning from this opportunity. End each session with feeling the fulfillment of success running through your senses. Studies published by Psychology Today, Forbes, Harvard

Business Review and more have established visualization as a powerful tool for ensuring success.

6. Implement reward moments for every success, of any magnitude. As a preemptive measure to start breaking the imposter cycle, establish a pattern of celebrating yourself for each success. It can be anything from an afternoon at the spa to a weekend away with women friends. This is a guarantee that you will have time and focus to internalize your accomplishments.

Neuroscience teaches us that brain activity is intimately intertwined with mental processes and human behavior patterns. When we shift our behaviors, we reset patterns of mindset. What this helps us understand is that adopting new activity responses when experiencing familiar discomfort interrupts cycles of habitual behavior. Introducing new responses to old internal accusations of being an imposter creates a pattern interruption that helps us break a habit or state of mind. The capacity to become bold and audacious leaders within our own lives, rests right in our own neurological patterns. Each of these practices presented in this chapter are designed to achieve this condition.

Imposter Syndrome is the result of our believing the self-diminishing thoughts that get triggered within our mind. *What if you simply change the script*, is an approach I've been teaching for many years. Changing our language, how we speak with ourselves, changes the way our brain responds to life. Resetting our human behavioral patterns is possible by doing something as simple as changing the outcome in our 'what if's'. Studies in brain science reveal this as a completely reasonable approach. Mindset reset can change the trajectory of our entire lives. What we hear, see and experience in a regular and consistent rhythm forms the basis of our belief system. We have been successfully talking ourselves into corners with negative self-speak for our entire lives. Conversely, we can lead ourselves into fulfillment of our greatest dreams through the exact same process, albeit redirected.

Shifting from *"what if I fail, what if this is a disaster,"* to *"what if I alter the entire process by approaching it as an adventure? What if I end up discovering satisfaction in my work?"* opens the neurological pathways to new potentials. *"What if I do achieve my goal? What if I do succeed? What if, I discover I know so much more than I've given myself credit for, up to this moment? What if, I dare, and in that I discover I am so much more than my dearest imagining? And, what if in the process I unknowingly give another woman permission to write a new story for herself, by modeling different behaviors?"*

Self-Sabotage

Self-sabotage is often expressed as an extension of *Imposter Syndrome*. Smart, even brilliant women with rich skill sets find themselves trapped in these cycles, women who are capable of so much more than what they are allowing themselves. Many women hold far greater vision than what they are revealing to their immediate circles or a limited social media audience. Locking themselves into habits or self-expressions that naturally distance others from them is a common tactic. These are often the very people who would otherwise be happy to open doors or present opportunities. Others do push through to achieve great heights but at the cost of their emotional comfort and peace of mind.

We've all grown up hearing the words, *"you're your own worst enemy"*. This is both the cost and purpose of self-sabotage. To understand how this is true, let's break it down a bit by looking at habits rooted in self-sabotage and their resulting toll on our lives.

Clinging to the past makes life feel stagnant. This applies to the good and bad moments. The happy moments can become pinnacles to which everything going forward must measure up. If not, the new experiences fall into some lesser category. Whatever joy is available is usurped by the comparison. Sad and unhappy to truly awful past moments ensure that you remain on high alert. This is especially activated by situations bearing the potential to lock you into all-too-familiar feelings from past events. Good or bad, holding onto the past is a promise to yourself to avoid centering in the now. This results in a fractured attention span and overlooking important details. It causes you to lose out on opportunities that your distracted state kept you from noticing. *Imposter Syndrome* at play, represented through self-sabotage.

Protecting your comfort zone is an active stance against growth. *"It's already been done." "That's not how it's done,"* are red flags that you are willing to forego many opportunities to maintain your status quo. And the ever-popular, *"I'm so far out of the box I don't even know where it is,"* is frequently a commitment to uniqueness for the sake of uniqueness. Avoiding anything that does not let you stand out, shine brighter, or feel 'more' than those around you, is its own expression of a comfort zone. Follow your gut, not tradition. Listen to your intuit, not your resistance. Let your innermost truth be your guide. It is your most authentic level of self and will never lead you into self-sabotage.

Relinquishing responsibility for life's potholes that you trip into is always self-sabotage. *"If they would just...the industry doesn't...people don't...if people would only..."* are all deflections of responsibility for personal choices. Or in some cases it is a resistance to choosing. Focusing outside of yourself for points of projection when life is not unfolding in the way you want, is a transference of your power onto an uncontrollable force. Conversely, if you dare a close examination, it will reveal what you are not doing to forward your own goals. This is practiced by many women. With surprising frequency I see it exhibited by those who present as having the world by the tail. They know they are exceptionally smart, talented and gutsy. In fear of being seen as anything less, therein an imposter, they struggle against taking ownership of their mis-steps. Subsequently they self-sabotage by externalizing responsibility for what they long for but lack. Stop and look within. Make a list of actions you can take, starting today. Create another list for the best and worst that can happen. This will help you recognize the fears you are holding between you and your internal comfort.

Engaging in perpetual self-appraisal over self-observation and self-acceptance will always sabotage your efforts. Picking yourself apart, dissecting your actions in search of flaws, scrutinizing how you performed below your capacity is the antithesis of self-acceptance. Rather it is self-sabotage driven by the fear of being found out as an imposter. Shifting to observation for the purpose of noticing what you can learn is wisdom. It recenters your focus on all that you are, subsequently derailing the feelings that rise to say that you are a fraud.

Not managing your expectations is a guarantee that they will manage you, right into the center of self-doubt and frustration. Remembering that an expectation is a belief, not a promise is a good starting place. Expectation rests in the assumption that a specific outcome will result from your actions. We all know where assumptions land us. Right in the center of self-sabotage, feeling like a fraud. Give yourself time. Allow for shifts in direction. Relax and breathe when encountering a snafu. Notice what is available to learn from the experience. It will prepare you to make different choices in the next round. Then start again with a calmed mind.

Self-sabotage through micromanagement is clinging to ideas of what you want and the exact steps in which it absolutely must happen. This stifles creativity and innovation. Yours, your team's, your family's, your organization's. Letting go is not the same as giving up. Lightening up on yourself allows you to do the same for all around you.

Not taking the time for self-nurturing experiences sends a message throughout your being that you are undeserving. Simple self-care is beneficial. But taking it to the next level of actual nurturance is a great derailer of self-sabotage. Nurturing yourself is a physical, emotional, mental, psychic reminder of how profoundly valuable you are, to yourself. Regular reminders of this nature help unravel *Imposter Syndrome*, thereby stifling the temptation to sabotage yourself.

Self-sabotage is instrumental in sustaining an *Imposter Syndrome* belief system. So, letting go of the habitual behaviors that feed it produces a great emancipation. As to self-sabotage, triple-board certified clinical and forensic neuropsychologist and tenured Associate Professor of Psychology at Pepperdine University. Dr. Judy Ho, Ph. D., ABPP, ABPdN, CFMHE, explains:

"We are essentially programmed to strive for goals because achieving them makes us feel good. That dopamine rush is an incentive to repeat those behaviors. The trick, especially when it comes to self-sabotage, is that our biochemistry doesn't necessarily discriminate between the kind of feel-good sensations we experience when we are going toward our goals and the 'good' feelings we get when we avoid something that seems threatening....."

Dopamine has been called our messenger molecule. It allows certain nerve cells in the brain to communicate with one another. It serves the functions within our central nervous system including pleasure and focus. The effects it has on our moods are powerful. This is why dopamine can inadvertently be our great enabler. As we revisit stories from our past, dopamine gratification falsely verifies our victimhood. It can produce a sense of survivor pride, but that rush is not sustainable. Only setting the stories down to live right here, in this moment, celebrating who we have become will position us to live a full life.

Our comfort zones feel familiar. Successfully protecting them can elicit a dopamine rush of satisfaction. This restricts us from setting ourselves free to discover the exhilaration available in realizing our potential. The supremacy of judgment, superiority, condemnation of those who have betrayed, maligned or worst of all, overlooked us, can keep us high on dopamine rushes. Only revisiting those accusations will allow the state to continue. Boldly claiming responsibility for every choice, action, mis-step and success will bestow sovereignty. Picking ourselves to pieces can produce a distorted self-satisfaction. Being proven right about our wrongness, can mean we dodged a bullet. Only we know the truth of our status as an imposter. With that relief, a release of dopamine can help us rise another day, but we will still carry the fear of being found out. Getting off our own backs and practicing observation for the purpose of learning will unlock our inner wisdom. It will breathe life-giving oxygen into all of our cells.

Each expression of Imposter Syndrome that is supported by self-sabotage will confirm that you are a fraud. That is a high price to pay for being right about something that drives anxiety through your entire body. On the surface self-sabotage doesn't make sense, but it doesn't live on the surface. It's a survival mechanism that helps us hide our deepest scars and fears. This is why it's so prevalent. We all have fears, and we each carry some wounds. So, one of the kindest things you can do for yourself is not add further damage via self-judgment about its presence in your life. Since it hasn't magically disappeared yet, it's completely reasonable to imagine it isn't going to do so now. Notice it, observe how you play it out and become aware of specific triggers. Ceasing to be afraid of looking yourself straight in the mirror, even on what you might call your 'bad days' is a step toward real freedom. Most importantly, be generous with yourself. Setting down a habit this well formed is going to take a minute.

Chapter Eleven

"Inclusivity means not 'just we're allowed to be there,' but we are valued. I've always said: smart teams will do amazing things, but truly diverse teams will do impossible things."

~ *Claudia Brind-Woody*

WOMEN DRIVING GENDER-DIVERSITY

For the past two decades women have led the movement toward greater values-based purchasing. The rising economic power they now possess is requiring companies to re-evaluate everything they sell and how it is marketed. The demands of busy executives, professionals, entrepreneurs, and mothers has been the inspiration for expansion in old industries and development of new ones. Personal style shopper networks are everywhere. Apps that send your grocery list directly to the market with delivery-request or designated pick-up time are becoming the norm. There has been an explosion of fashion, beauty and self-care products customized to fill the needs of women of differing races and cultures.

Additionally, women are using their new standard of economic power to shortcut as many unpaid labor tasks as possible. Busy women are looking for convenience. They have deserved it for a long time and more women daily are factoring it into the budget as a justifiable expense. Over the past several years the sentiment, *"if you want to know where the market is going, follow the women,"* has repeatedly been presented in many of our top business magazines. Scrutinizing how merchandise is produced and by what means, has forced company leaders to do the same. Concurrently, they are having to adjust their marketing strategies at a pace never before witnessed.

This same trend is spawning a growing number of female-owned, founded and operated businesses. This is a considerable demonstration of women working in alliance. More women are

179

feeling empowered to start their own companies based on a single understanding. They are women. Therefore, they understand other women. They have spent years or decades complaining with their friends about products that would make their lives more comfortable but that have never made it to the market. Similarly, they can all cite the design flaws in products made for women, by men. Two notable examples; a functional handbag and jeans with pockets deep enough for more than a breath mint. For this same reason they understand how to develop marketing strategies that speak to women. The custom of marketers objectifying or speaking down to the female populace is falling to its rightful place. Extinction. All of this is driving gender diversity within the broader marketplace. Talented female designers not interested in owning their own businesses are a huge asset to teams that produce products for women, from clothes and bags to personal care and beauty.

This growth is not limited to woman-centric products. Even companies producing household tools are placing greater value on the input of their female team members. After all, it is still women who both purchase and use them the majority of the time. Companies paying attention to language trends, evolving cultural perceptions, and burgeoning social attitudes are generating increased female customer loyalty. Just as are companies who provide exceptional service and purchasing experiences. Those building a strong public awareness of their gender equality initiatives, are seeing momentous gains in the number of loyal female customers.

Another area in which women's power has been underutilized is within leadership roles of the traditional workplace. They regularly find their unique insights and contributions dismissed, out-of-hand. It is not unusual for a woman to learn, a few days after the fact, that the company has adopted the proposal of a male colleague. The decision maker's justification being that on close examination, the woman's strategy showed less potential. It is generally known that the striking similarities between the proposals are a verboten topic.

We are seeing an ever increasing number of women who have earned their stripes, suffered their emotional bruises and are fed-up with the status quo. Translating their hard-earned skills into entrepreneurship is a natural step. Highly educated and talented women like Janine Hamner-Holman from chapter 4, are finding both financial and personal fulfillment through independent consultancy. These same women are building intentional Women's Alliance Groups. The support of colleagues meeting on a monthly basis fills the interactional void created by leaving a large organization. The absence of a single company shingle is an equalizer that emboldens each member to freely share their best tips. We all need cheerleaders, something that's too often absent within competitive company cultures.

The following chart gives insight to the expansions taking place in the world of women's business:

According to Fundera of NYC

- *The US has **12.3 million** women-owned businesses.*

- *US women-owned businesses generate **$1.8 trillion** a year.*

- ***40%** of US businesses are women-owned.*

- *Women started **1,821** net new businesses every day last year. (in spite of a worldwide pandemic)*

- ***64%** of new women-owned businesses were started by women of color last year.*

- *Latina owned businesses grew more than **87%**.*

- *There are **114%** more women entrepreneurs than there were 20 years ago.*

- ***62%** of women entrepreneurs cite their business as their primary source of income.*

- *Private tech companies led by women achieve **35%** higher ROI. [Return on investment]*

- *Women-founded companies in First Round Capital's portfolio outperformed companies founded by men by **63%**.*

- *Just **25%** of women business owners seek business financing.*

- *Women receive just **7%** of venture funds for their startups.*

- *Women have a **69.5%** success rate of crowdfunding for their businesses while men have a **61.4%** success rate.*

- ***57.4%** of the SBA Microloan program's loans went to women-owned or women-led businesses.*

There is more research coming forward quarterly which is indicating that female business owners are setting a new pace in diversity and inclusion programs, which is an understandable trend based on their having been too long on the wrong side of the equality scale. While the data is still out, there is both growing and reasonable speculation that this dedication to female equity and diversity is the factor driving their higher gains over other new businesses. Another advantage women are discovering is getting officially certified as a woman owned business on federal and local levels. Large corporations and multiple levels of government are the largest buyers of goods and services in the US. The growing attention to diversity has highly motivated them to consistently award contracts to women owned businesses. These contracts can become constant and reliable sources of revenue to support company growth.

One would be hard pressed to find any top business magazine that has not published multiple articles on women's superior leadership skills. Those forward-thinking companies leading the movement to hire and promote more women are showing quantifiable upswings in both their organizational growth and quarterly profits. Yet inexplicably, women do not find their numbers within the executive suites increasing at a pace equaling their positive reviews.

For women possessed of a natural inclination toward leadership, who are tired of being passed over for less talented men, entrepreneurship and business ownership are viable options. Often, the only missing component is the courage to audaciously go for it. This is an area where surrounding oneself with powerful female alliances can be the motivating ingredient. The female entreprencur or business owner who has not known her fair share of doubts is as rare as snow in the Mojave. It's not a matter of whether or not fears exist. They have, they do, and they will. The question is how to reinforce oneself against letting them dominate. The other thing female leaders will tell any woman with a dream is; the fulfillment of independence always outweighs the challenges. It has been my experience as well as that of the many female entrepreneurs and business owners I've spoken with, that each victory builds the confidence we need to succeed by factors of 10 to 100 or more.

Women Create Diversity Rich Environments

Woman-owned businesses experiencing applaudable growth rates are creating more opportunities for all women. It can open doors to high-level mentoring relationships with other women who are already succeeding in entrepreneurship. Finding a work environment that best suits the needs of their greater life has always challenged women. Business ownership allows them the authority to create their own scenario. Skills that were either taken for granted or depreciated within male-driven companies can be fully utilized to create independent success. Women of color, long undervalued, are making exciting strides to equalize their families and socio-economic status through business ownership.

The long-established fact that women are natural collaborators is paying off in these new endeavors. Those building woman-owned, women-operated businesses are creating entire cultures in which women are thriving. Their level of collaborative success is the result of the inclusion of women from every stratum of the racial, cultural spectrum, and represents a level of innovation that can only be reaped from a broad circle of perspectives and influences.

At the end of everyday a business's success or failure comes down to leadership style. The increase of women's voices in corporate, C-Suite, and politics have served to establish that women have notable talent for leading. They know how to identify the goal and execute action-plans that deliver. Having mastered time-management during their years of balancing the home-work demand, they are prepared for the rigors of leadership. Women are assembling teams capable of tracking and meeting their quarterly key point indicators, and bringing a project to completion on time and on budget.

In his presentation at Inc.'s Women's Summit, Kevin O' Leary of *Shark Tank* fame spoke of his preference for investing in woman-owned businesses. He cited the reason as being that they produce superior returns. Of the more than 40 companies he's invested in, close to 95% of the women-led companies met their financial targets, compared with just 65% of the businesses headed by male leaders.

News of women's talent for leadership is spreading. There is a growing awareness of the more diversity driven, inclusion focused cultures they are creating within large to monolithic companies. This translates into expanding opportunities for those women not wanting to build their own business. Research from Berlin Cameron, The Harris Poll and The Female Quotient, reveals that:

> *"...half of Americans would prefer to work for a female-led company over a male-led company, including 46% of men. It also found that 71% of both men and women feel that having a woman in a leadership position makes them believe that they too can achieve a leadership position."*

Gender Equality

There is no disputing that gender equality is a complex goal. One that has produced many perspectives and ideologies. The question of which will produce the most long-range and unifying results has generated as much dialogue as any issue in business. The prevailing reality is that fostering equality so that all people can claim their inherent right to sustainably, fulfilling lives is a moral imperative. It is the single *humane* choice.

Gender equality is not just a women's issue. Men will also benefit. Women represent all races, cultures, religious affiliations and sexual orientations. As a new ethos of equality and equity for all trickles down, every community from elders to our current generation of children and those to come will be positively impacted. The up-leveling of our greater society will touch every aspect from healthcare and education, to financial fluidity. While not the sum and substance of why we need equality, studies show that gender diversity generates increased earnings. A recent study conducted by Institute for Women's Leadership, Nichols College revealed:

- *U.S. women represent 47% of the workforce and in 40% of families, women are the primary or sole breadwinner.*

- *Companies in the top quartile for gender diversity are 15% more likely to outperform the competition.*

Gender equality will bring about more diverse political representation for all people. Increased political power for women of all races, cultures, sexual orientations and religions will position them to forward initiatives toward diversity, equality, inclusion and fair distribution of equity. For our world to thrive it is imperative that we begin empowering the intrinsic humanity of all people with personal dignity. Correspondingly, it is necessary that we are each provided with actionable equity. The absence of equity cripples the pursuit of equality.

As of 2017, gender equality was the fifth of seventeen sustainable development goals (SDG 5) of the United Nations. Gender equality will produce across-the-board equal outcomes for women, men and gender-diverse people of all religions, races, cultures, and sexual orientations. This has been an ongoing quest dating back through many ages. So how do we now pick up the thread and proceed with renewed determination?

The Power of Empathy

The higher empathy quotient inherent to women is naturally creating company cultures that honor a broader range of voices and perspectives. Women have been taught to suppress empathy by having it cited as a weakness. Both the business and political realms have condemned women as a whole, accusing them of excessive emotionality. In truth empathy is a far more elevated expression. In a recent study comparing women's capacity for empathy to men's Dr. Marco Iacoboni, director of the Neuromodulation Lab at the UCLA Ahmanson-Lovelace Brain Mapping Center reported:

"Our data suggest that females are better at feeling others' pain, at really getting the feeling that the other person is having right now. Female participants in the study showed relatively higher activation in a sensory area of the brain associated with pain than their male counterparts."

Women's natural access to empathy grants them broader perspectives. From that vantage point they derive more all-inclusive interpretations of situations. Due to the overwhelming load women have carried in supporting a functional society, they are masters at dealing with changes, up to the last possible minute. Necessity has demanded this of them. The result is a finer attunement to the quiet inner voice that produces breakthrough results. Not the least of these inner guidance systems is empathy. Combining empathy with their early imprinting to assume excessive responsibility, inclines women to break down barriers rather than construct them. Rebalancing the overload, or redistributing portions of it, gives them the time and emotional bandwidth to offer more attention to themselves. The result is increased energy to share freely with each other. The potential benefits of women bringing their finely attuned senses together through alliance are limitless. Through the numerous mutations of COVID-19 that extended our recent global pandemic, that was more important than ever before. The effects of the pandemic touched everything in our lives and more severely impacted women's obligations. Families, community engagements, other women, business and the struggle for cultural evolution were affected. Studies indicate it may be a decade before we understand the true cost that the pandemic leveled upon our world society.

The nationwide collapse of child-care centers is just one of the issues women with children will be called to remedy. A report from the Center for American Progress and the Century Foundation, reveals that the child-care crisis could cost women $64.5 billion per year in lost wages. This is one of the many areas in which women can be of considerable support to one another by creating networks of alliance. Not to care for each other's children. Rather, to mindshare toward new and innovative solutions for themselves and each other. The results of this will inevitably impact our greater society in a positive direction.

Numerous studies have revealed that the historical practice of isolating women is the surest way to disempower them. The pandemic resulted in the longest periods of social isolation in modern history. It is no surprise that the statistics shared through hundreds of sources confirm that during that extended confinement women assumed an even greater workload. Upgrading their tech skills to include online schooling and becoming the primary teacher to their children are notable examples. All of this with less support than what they were previously able to access, due to protracted quarantine restrictions followed by stresses on businesses attempting to regain their footing. We are yet to discover the multitude of ways in which there is no normal, no old world to which we will return. There has been no time in recent history when women's voices, ingenuity, ability to pivot on a dime and capacity for empathy have been more vital. In spite of the additional time and energy investments, many women are already on task to co-create potential resolutions. With all its unprecedented challenges and heartbreaking losses, we are facing a unique opportunity to create a more equanimous world for everyone.

Coupling and Parenting for Equality

During an interview for their book, *Good Guys: How Men Can Be Better Allies for Women in the Workplace*, authors David G Smith and W Brad Johnson said:

"Women told us that gender equality at work had to start with men becoming equal partners at home. Real allyship and gender partnership demands that men do their fair share of household chores, childcare, transportation for children's activities, the emotional labor of planning and tracking activities, and supporting their partner's career."

There is true progress being made toward more equitable distribution of responsibilities within new generation families. Of the almost 250 interviews I've conducted with women over the past three years, more than 100 were members of the Gen-Z and younger end of the Millennial demographics. Many couples from these groups have already adopted progressive lifestyle patterns. A new standard was adopted, from the onset, referring to each other as partners versus earlier generations' use of the terms husband and wife. This intentional choice was based on viewing the old terms as antiquated expressions of ownership. They feel 'partner' immediately sets the tenor of their relationships in a direction of equality. Those who cohabitate prior to marriage (the standing majority) continue the pre-established patterns of who will cook, do laundry, etc., and on which days, into their marriage. Although not their primary objective, they have modeled these behaviors for couples who did not live together prior to marriage. Subsequently, the new measure of engaged responsibility for the home is spreading throughout these generations.

For those who chose to parent, all the responsibilities of childcare and rearing are shared equally. It's no longer the man 'helping out' with the kids and home. Likewise, it isn't just mommy carpooling, driving the soccer team or arranging every doctor and dental appointment. Three of the women spoke of how watching same-sex couples within their circles had informed the development of their own coparenting styles. The lesbian couples interviewed who are co-parenting, shared how completely natural it feels to distribute responsibilities for the family, equally.

A fully engaged acknowledgement that the children, home and their associate needs fall to both parents appears to be producing a more cohesive family foundation. The relationship between the parents is enhanced and they are able to maintain their intimate connection. All the parents reported a deep sense of satisfaction about being fully present in their children's lives. Many referenced having received far less attention from their hard-working fathers. Their own parenting roles had begun with a commitment to give their children something they had not received and feel is irreplaceable, the time and devoted attention of two fully engaged parents. *Familying*, a word I coined to describe how these couples are parenting, has become an all players on deck team sport.

Building marriage-equity is a shared experience of true significance. Nurturing communicatively engaged relationships is a top priority for these generations of women and clearly, their seniors who are ahead of the curve. Regardless of age or generation, each of the women experiencing equality in their relationship are clear that the old tradition of marriage by rote holds no fascination.

As per specific studies presented in chapter 5, there is also a growing number of men taking over the responsibility for the home and kids, by retiring to become househusbands. Contrary to outdated beliefs, the emotional health and thriving scholastic accomplishments of these children reveal that stay-at-home dads can be as well suited to this role as any woman. Additional studies reveal some male parents can be more prepared for this role than a mother who is naturally endowed with the drive for professional excellence. Most importantly, the children being raised in these environments are experiencing a whole new approach to life, partnering and parenting. As they grow to adulthood, they are poised to become valuable leaders in progressing our society toward the long-coveted goal of equality.

My interviews with baby boomers and Gen X women revealed that many men of these generations are also becoming more proactive partners within the home. For most, their kids are graduate students or living established adult lives that have produced grandchildren now in their late teens. Yet the fathers/grandfathers engagement with their wives/partners daily experiences and everything required to create a sustainable non-work life has assumed a new level of priority. Within these more forwardly-responsive partnerships, women are finding themselves emancipated from inequitable emotional burdens. A growing number of studies reveal that women with equal partners at home are more successful at work. The results of this research serves as yet another indicator of the positive impact equality can afford our entire society.

Gender Bias

During children's educational experience gender related divisions are expressed by teachers, administrators and mirrored to one another. The percentage of attention paid to historical male figures outdistances what is given to women of history to a deplorable degree. Not seeing the plethora of female change-makers and trailblazers who lived before has a profoundly negative effect on our girl's developing self-images. Further, the idea of their fragility is relayed in numerous manners. Girls are handled much more severely for fighting and labeled with the term 'bad girls'. This is not leveled as a judgment of their actions but of their fundamental being. On the flip side there is an expectation that boys will fight. That is spoken of as boys just being boys and learning to toughen up in preparation for manhood.

From these well-established frameworks our young people are fully indoctrinated with unconscious bias by the time they reach university age. The girls are deeply convinced of their inferior status as humans and the boys are fully programmed to believe in their intrinsic superiority. There has been ongoing conversation around equalizing the treatment of our male and female children for decades. Yet there is still little pro-active movement in this direction. Our own unconscious bias is the obvious hurdle in recognizing how to accomplish this for our youth. This is one area where we, as women, can align to take a more assertive role. Women birth 100% of the children. According to recent statistics from PEW Research Center, one-in-four mothers are raising children on their own. For those with partners, eight-in-ten women, 77%, are the primary parent of influence. It is time for women to lead the charge in implementing programs that teach our children from early in their youth about the equality of all genders. Educating a future generation of adults in equality literacy will require more of us to develop that language within ourselves. Therein the benefits to be reaped will start immediately.

To successfully address gender inequality and gender inequity it is essential to define the behaviors exemplifying a presence of gender bias. As most women know from experience, gender bias is prejudicial behavior that empowers one gender over another. Our societal standards that serve to enable gender bias see males promoted over females. This is represented in realms ranging from business to politics. Over the past few years the Hollywood pay gap has come under much deserved public scrutiny. The attitude of men's enhanced worth begins from birth. An example generally taken for granted is the difference in the way male babies can receive the father's legacy in the form of Jr, or III. While a female child may be named after an ancestor, this rarely comes with the same honorarium. Even in 2022 there are families in which inheritances continue to be primarily bestowed on the male offspring with the assumption he will distribute to the females with ongoing oversight.

While the behavior of gender bias is ancient, the cultural terminology is a fairly recent addition to the lexicon. Consequently, this is why it is often (and incorrectly) used in place of the more familiar, sexism.

Sexism: prejudice or discrimination based on sex

Gender bias: the differential treatment of males and females, based on stereotypes and not real differences

As we see, sexism is based in theory, where gender bias is the behavior expressed in compliance with fixed and oversimplified ideas around that theory. Therein, the necessary condition for gender bias is sexism while the bias itself presents in the form of behaviors that expose the core prejudice.

On the surface some may assume that only females suffer due to gender bias, when in fact it also takes a notable toll on men, families and all sectors of society. Consider the great cost to men and children of losing their wife, partner, or mother due to the lack of sufficient attention being given to women's health. Or, the lingering financial devastation following a lengthy illness suffered by a female family member, be they a mother, senior, or daughter. Each situation is a poignant example of the cost to our society caused by an imbalance of financial endowments dedicated to women's health studies.

During COVID we all witnessed one of the vaccines pulled from the market following deaths due to blood clots. Of the 7 million shots that had been received by that time, 6 produced a tragic result. I have no criticism of the decision to pull it from distribution. I am certainly not minimizing the loss to the families of the 6 women who died. Instead, I use this situation as a point of comparison, only. For the past 50+ years birth control pills have been known to cause blood clots in 1 in 1000 women. They have faced the choice of taking the chance of not being the *one* or giving birth to babies they do not want, for reasons they should not have to explain. Even more devastating is when they find themselves pregnant with a child they can't afford or are not emotionally prepared to parent. Then consider the years it took for women's birth control to be accepted, let alone covered by health insurance. Conversely, the same insurance companies adopted Viagra almost concurrently to its arrival on the market and in 2020 it received $46.1M in dedicated federal funding.

One key reason for women's health issues taking a distant backseat to men's in the world of research, is the degree to which girls are discouraged from pursuing careers in medicine. The small but growing increase of females in the industry is already demonstrating a pivot toward better and more focused research into women's health. Yet the situation is still dire. According to a report from Becker's Hospital Review, little more than 1 million professionally active physicians are currently practicing in the U.S.. Females represent 359,409 of our current physician base. This translates to a gender ratio gap of 1.8 male physicians to 1 female physician.

How many great female doctors might we gain by dismantling the gender bias programming that female children are subjected to from birth? How many innovative approaches to medicine and medical research could be developed to save millions of lives through their unique way of viewing challenges? At the very least, how many people could be made more comfortable during a protracted illness by encouraging qualified female students to pursue careers in medicine and offering them an equal platform for learning?

Gender Equity

Women are natural equity builders. In many cases, they just haven't realized this or known how to utilize it. They possess established equity within their circles who don't hesitate to call them in moments of question, confusion or need. If they are mothers, they have built equity with everyone from the doctor who always takes their call or returns it promptly, to educators, sports coaches, other moms, and more. If they are not parents, they have still spent the surplus hours creating an equity base. This extends from house-sitters to the local wine merchant who always sets aside a bottle from the shipment of their favorite vintage.

Some may respond to this overview with, "but that doesn't pay the mortgage." Maybe not directly, but let's take a closer look. How much time and money are reclaimed into a woman's day through these alliances? But, are they legitimate alliances? Each individual you can turn to for support, counsel, or an advantage that may benefit in a number of applications is a type of alliance partner. As has been established women are disinclined to ask for a favor until they've first figured out what they can give in return. It will serve women to start viewing their accumulated relational assets from a clarified perspective. Who does the wine shop owner know that you should know? The relationship has been long established through loyal customership. There need not be any fear of a lingering debt to repay. Start noticing the alliances that already exist. Asking a question as non-confrontational as, *who do you know that I should know*" could produce surprisingly favorable results.

One way women build equity, second only to their careers, is by showing other women how to fill their own equity banks. There is little that establishes more equity at a faster pace, than sharing its benefits. Refocusing on associations as people with whom you share equity benefits everyone. Women are imprinted to be helpful and skilled problem solvers. As they begin applying equity building and sharing throughout their social circles a rhythm of mutually supportive self-image building is established. Not all female Alliance Groups need to be formal. Non-professional circles are an equity-rich environment that most women, including some professionals, don't recognize as an expression of wealth.

Women view their non-work relationships through a different lens than men. It is as natural as walking into a room for men to commoditize their relationships. An approach the majority of women find fundamentally distasteful, to the extent of never engaging in such activity. A recent article in PsychCentral compared the difference between male-male and female-female relationship styles:

> ".... women tend to prefer more friendship-relationships. ... Friendships between males tend to be more side-to-side rather than face-to-face. Males tend to value relationships that include shared activities...and are transactional..."

Certainly, I am not suggesting that women need to become more transactional. The nurture-based, empathy-rich approach to relationships that women express is a vital facet of who they are. Further, it is an expression of their authentic power. What I am inviting women to consider more broadly is how they are undervaluing their contributions, and the degree to which this is limiting their overall lives. This encouragement speaks particularly to non-career-based beneficence.

Due to the volume of equity women do not put into play, let's take an elucidative view into what it is and what it can be used to accomplish. In application to gender the word equity refers to fairness and justice. In and of itself, it does not render equality. However, establishing equity is a prerequisite toward experiencing equal status. As a stand-alone, equality means providing the same to all. As a counterpart, equity is the recognition that we do not all start from the same place. Achieving equality requires acknowledging the imbalances and taking the necessary actions to adjust for them.

To illustrate the imbalances within gender equality and equity, respected business coach, Jackie Nagle, compiled the following chart that makes the disparity easier to visualize.

Women are 50.8% of the population.

Women hold 59% of master's degrees.

Women hold 57% of undergraduate degrees.

Women are 47% of the US labor force.

For white women 'Equal Pay Day' is celebrated on March 31.

Equal Pay Day for black women will be on August 13

Equal Pay Day for Latina women on Oct. 29

Meaning:

The average white woman had to work 3 additional months into 2020 in order to earn as much as the average man in the US in 2019.

The average black woman had to work just over twice that many additional months, 71/2, into 2020 in order to earn as much as the average man in the US in 2019.

The average Latina woman had to work a full 10 additional months into 2020 in order to earn as much as the average man in the US in 2019.

The issue of equity must be addressed in order to offer all women equal footing. Another oppressor of women Ms. Nagle's chart clearly demonstrates is the disparity of equity between white women and women of color. Is time for white women to take a lead in this area by becoming proactively inclusive. It is impossible to imagine how much incredible talent we are losing by viewing employment candidates through the lens of racial bias.

As to the subject of workplace equity, the following are excerpts from a recently published Harvard Business Review article: *"Gender Equity Is Not Zero Sum"* by Katica Roy, David G. Smith, W. Brad Johnson.

"Businesses that commit to closing their gender equity gaps across all races and ethnicities enjoy increased profitability and returns on equity, productivity, and innovation; a greater ability to attract and retain top talent; and revenue gains."

Research by Pipeline, for whom Katica Roy serves as CEO, revealed that:

"For every 10% increase in gender equity, businesses see a 1% to 2% increase in revenue."

Their conclusion being:

"We cannot afford to wait centuries for men to fully engage as accomplices and advocates in achieving full gender parity in the workplace, especially at a time when our economic recovery depends on the equitable inclusion of employees."

The workplace is a key arena where women have resisted forming strong alliances. Some are motivated by a fear of losing what they perceive as the only seat at the table. For others it is the fear of being overtaken by a talented junior female colleague. As long as we cling to the internalized misogyny that provokes us to malign other women, we will all lose. If we continue to imagine limited real estate, that is all that will be available to women. Perpetuating fear of our younger female colleagues equals forfeiting any chance to learn from their innovative perspectives. We cannot suppress them and simultaneously gain their understanding of how to market to new generations of buyers. I would argue that our greatest loss in these competitions is equity. Specifically, that gained by empowering each other to reach our greatest potentials. Loyalty is another form of equity. Lifting our younger professionals up onto our seasoned shoulders is powerfully enriching. Sharing wisdom that can only be gained from years of experience, is a gift to both women. Significantly, it seeds in our junior associate a new standard of woman-to-woman relationship within the business world. When replicated in large numbers this will become the legacy that we pass to our daughters and granddaughters.

Becoming Comfortable with Discomfort

One of the most important benefits of building alliances is the way these group interactions can bring us face to face with thoughts, beliefs and habits we have long struggled to acknowledge.

I can't say when the realization hit that my single path to enjoying the life I'd chosen was to learn to be comfortable with discomfort. Certainly, since that time I've encountered many words on the topic offered by wise and thoughtful people. All of which fed my understanding that this was not unique to me, but rather an invitation life offers each of us. Sitting comfortably in my discomfort required learning to ask hard questions. The irony is that once asked and answered, more questions appear. It's a continuum of learning, and one in which we are all being asked to engage more enthusiastically. From the boardroom to the corner cafés, we are in need of asking questions that reflect the limitations in our perceptions. From there we must remain emotionally open to hearing the answers. Learning to appreciate our differences and how they enrich us as a whole is the single means of broadening understanding.

The alarming events we have been witnessing across the country are affecting each person in a different way and to varying degrees. Racial injustice, culture diverse motivated hate crimes, and unequal distribution of power and equity exist across the board. Each of these is impacting women deeply. Mothers are wrenched with justifiable concern for their children's safety each time they leave the home. Across the age spectrum, women are watching the right to make choices about their own bodies slip away. The inability to speak with each other, to calmly hear viewpoints that differ from our own, has risen to ear-splitting proportions. Engaging in uncomfortable conversations with the goal of understanding has never been more imperative. It's time to get to know colleagues, community members, and people different from ourselves. We are surrounded by opportunities daily, from our jobs to our social lives. Endeavoring to understand another human allows us to become invested in their job and financial security as well as their greater life. We experience ourselves having an emotional stake in their personal safety. When we hold the power to do so, we are quicker to advocate for another woman when she's unjustifiably bypassed for promotions. If not sufficiently positioned, we can find ourselves more inclined to help her brainstorm new options. Our senses become attuned to the words that diminish our female peers. A new level of responsibility for our actions takes hold. Becoming comfortable with our discomfort lets us ask uncomfortable questions and remain present to hear the answers. This is an important and proactive step in becoming the best of ourselves.

Conversely, letting our discomfort take the role of repressing those conversations can inflict real harm. Never has there been more at risk for each of us. Which also means, never has there been more for us to gain, as we intentionally build collective alliances. Becoming comfortable with our own discomfort is essential to creating a society rooted in diversity, equity and inclusion, and anchored in empathy. While empathy is rarely listed alongside diversity, equity and inclusion, it is the active ingredient in amplifying and guiding the other three. Possessing the ability to understand and share the feelings of another provides the inspiration to shift from fear and judgment, into compassionate allyship.

Conclusion

"The world needs strong women. Women who will lift and build others, who will love and be loved. Women who live bravely, Women of indomitable will."

~ Amy Tenney, Human Rights Attorney

THE TIME OF THE WOMAN

As many before me have said; *"This is the time of the woman."* This truth rings out into every area of our culture and society, not just business. Social justice has seen an uprising of powerful women, spanning all cultures and demographics. Each is dedicating her voice and commitment to creating a more humane society. These new movements created by mighty women are calling focused attention to long-standing issues that have never been honestly addressed. Pulling back the veil has created a wave of momentum impossible to ignore. So much so that a visible percentage of men are actively engaging with these movements and the women who founded them. Consequently, vast numbers are being affected with the potential to impact even more.

My own commitment to social justice was born after hitchhiking to NYC during the second wave of the women's movement, what was then called, the Women's Liberation Movement. I would never dare to claim an impact as powerful as some of the familiar voices of that time or the young women we see stepping up today. Yet, as it was the younger and more energized of us then, again we see that it is the younger females of these new generations now taking up the mantle of their individual passions to serve the many.

Who of us will forget the poignantly excruciating 6 minutes and 20 seconds when Emma Gonzalez stood on that Washington DC stage in utter silence for all the world to *hear,* during The March for Our Lives? This was the precise amount of time it took a gunman to kill the 17 classmates whose names she spoke from that same stage.

Through this she is a standing inspiration to women of all generations of the power of impassioned commitment to justice.

At only 8-years-old, Amariyanna "Mari" Copen, known around the globe as Little Miss Flint, wrote a letter to President Barack Obama. She invited the then president to visit her home of Flint, MI to witness first-hand their dire need for clean, safe water. Mari continues to create dialogue around environmental racism and has become the voice for vast numbers of Americans trapped in collapsing toxic infrastructures. The list of her accomplishments on behalf of the underrepresented would be enviable for a 30 year old. Currently 14, Mari is already positioned as a respected voice of leadership.

Few don't know the name Malala Yousafzai, who in October of 2014, at only 17 years old was awarded a Nobel Prize for Peace. Years after having been shot in the head by the Taliban for speaking out for girl's education her commitment has never wavered. As she stated in 2015,

> *"There is nothing wrong with calling yourself a feminist. So I am a feminist, and we all should be feminists because feminism is another word for equality."*

When she was in elementary school Marley Dias realized the devastating impact of being black and a girl who never saw her own face or read her own story in books. Not willing to accept the main protagonist in most books as white boys, at 12, Marley founded an organization to collect and distribute books that featured black girls as the lead character. Now 16 and still in high school, she is a published author, has hosted a children's Netflix series, has distributed over 10,000 books worldwide and works toward social justice.

While I give honor to these younger women already at work for the greater good, what aren't and can't be named are the countless thousands of women hard at work to make the lives of others more gentle and more equal. Women are serving our debilitated elders, marginalized children and those in their own small communities who are challenged in a variety of ways. Some are seeding grassroots political movements around issues impeding the lives of citizens in their home states. Tens to hundreds of thousands of women are doing what they were trained since birth to do, and what comes naturally. They are giving care. Except now more of them are reaching out beyond the borders of their homes and families and doing so in bolder ways. It is predominantly women I see rising up to extinguish another national, sometimes international epidemic. The epidemic of 'ism'. Racism, ageism, sexism, tokenism, and all the other 'ism' representations of oppression. Whether one joins the movement to eliminate the 'isms' by replacing them with humane treatments of all people in a big way or a small way, it is time to take action.

What Feminism Is and Isn't

During my many years of working with women I've repeatedly heard the same statement. "I'm not a Feminist." Some went so far as to say, "I can't even stand the word." Asked why, the most common responses were, "I don't hate men," or "I don't think women are superior to men." This misconception is as old as the struggle for women's rights. It never ceases to surprise me how many women confuse an intolerance of toxic masculinity for an abhorrence of all men.

Equally bewildering is how many smart and educated women still foster antiquated and false beliefs that work against their own best interests. The perceptions I've heard about Feminists and Feminism range from, "We're equal, we have the power of the vote," to, "We have equal job opportunities and can choose any university we want to attend," to, "There's nothing stopping me from making my own decisions."

Another dated and yet still active belief is that Feminists want to shift the power balance to put women, and exclusively women, in all top leadership positions. The idea being that the ultimate goal of Feminism is to institute reverse inequality by placing all men in a position of subservience.

There are many men that I and other Feminist's love and respect. A significant majority of these men are actively aligning with the

Feminist movement, based on their understanding that its goal is not to subjugate them and that they too will reap great benefit from women's equality.

What has become glaringly apparent through these conversations is that many modern-day women are still uninformed as to what a Feminist and the intention of Feminism are. The amount of false information that those opposing equality pour into our media and society is a significant reason for why so many women have a hard time separating fact from fiction, in respect to what Feminism is and isn't.

As author and Feminist theorist *bell hooks* states clearly and frankly in her seminal book, *Feminism is for Everybody*,

"Feminism is a movement to end sexism, sexist exploitation, and oppression."

To further clarify, a Feminist is an individual who believes in Feminism and focuses their energy toward helping women achieve equal rights and fair equity. Further, they believe that equality and equity are the inherent right of *all* people.

Additional confusion rests in identifying whether Feminism is a purely political position or if it is a statement of personal values. This begs the recognition that just because women are asking to have protection of their rights outlined in the U.S. Constitution, does not mean it is only a political movement. The right to life, liberty and the pursuit of happiness are based in human value, and yet they are each named in the U.S. Constitution.

Due to the struggle to be granted Constitutionally dictated equal rights having been ongoing for women since 1868 when the 14th Amendment to the U.S. Constitution granted all persons (defined at that time as 'men' only) 'equal protection under the law,' many women see the struggle of Feminism as being outdated. The truth remains that 'equal protection under the law' for women has still not been written into the U.S. Constitution and its associate amendments.

Many who shun the terms Feminist and Feminism pose the argument that successful women such as Sheryl Sandberg, Indra Nooyi, and Arianna Huffington stand as examples of women's equality. While each of these are women of great vision, strength and accomplishment, they still represent the minority. When we look at Fortune 500 CEOs, in 2022 there are only 41 as opposed to 459 men. After the last election cycle there was great celebration that the number of women in Congress had risen to an all-time high of 27%. When we remember that women are a full 50.53% of the U.S. population, we see these numbers do not support the notion that women enjoy the privileges and protections offered through Constitutionally clarified equality.

So, what is the importance of women's equality?

It is true that we've had the vote since 1920. That was a mere 44 years after the 15th Amendment to the U.S. Constitution granted black *men* the right to vote. So yes, we have the right to vote, but this does not, in and of itself, place us in a position of equal.

As to the question of equal treatment of women in the workplace, let's look at the most recent statistics from Pew Research Center.

23% of women are more likely to be considered incompetent due to their gender.

Female workers are nearly four times as likely as their male colleagues to report being regarded as incompetent because of their gender. However, according to gender discrimination in the workplace statistics, only 6% of working men admitted they had received unfair treatment.

Similarly, 16% of working women said they repeatedly received minor insults in the workplace due to their gender. Those insults could be implicit, in the form of inadequate jokes or explicit comments directed at one's gender, physical appearance, or sexual orientation. In contrast, only 5% of men encountered such unpleasantries.

With women outdistancing men at 60% female, 40% male in university enrollment it is accurate to claim equality to educational access. The disparity shows up after graduation with men receiving an average 20% higher starting salary over equally educated women.

Gender equality stands as a means to legal protection in respect to violence against women and girls. The data is in from sources around the world revealing that gender equality and equity stimulate economic growth and produce societies that are safer and healthier for all citizens.

Another advantage of equality was revealed by a study conducted by McKinsey & Company Global Institute stating that a worldwide view shows that gender diverse companies are 15% more likely to out earn their competitors.

The understanding that every human has an essential right to live a life that is free from discrimination in every form is the origin of Amnesty International's statement that, *"Women's rights are human rights"*.

Great female leaders from bell hooks to author Chimamanda Ngozi Adichie and Justice Ruth Bader Ginsburg have long proclaimed, *"Feminism should and can benefit everyone"*.

Feminism and being a Feminist is not a fad, an intention to eliminate men, or a movement to try to force women into any particular role. It is a stance for women to have the absolute right to choose their own path and lifestyle. Whether a woman wants to be a stay-at-home mom or the leader of a great nation, Feminism is the struggle for her right to claim these personal goals, and Feminists are out in the world speaking up on behalf of all women to have the right to achieve these self-directed choices.

It is *our* time to rise and be loud, be bold, to be unapologetic in our demand for benevolent, equality, and equity in the lives of every person. This is *our* time to take up the words of Gandhi and, *"Be the change you want to see in the world."* It is *our* time to look around and give care that it is equal, just, equitable and above all, humane'. *This is our time.*

Acknowledgements

It is with unwavering gratitude to a great circle of women, and a few great men, that I was able to navigate the journey of bringing this passion driven work to fruition. Writing this book was its own circle of experience, filled with support and love.

To my publisher Juliet Clark, you have been amazing! From the beginning, your unfaltering enthusiasm for this book has been a source of assurance and encouragement. Through all the tangles inherent to the world of writing and publishing, I have remained grateful for your calm, consistency and generosity. The hoops you jumped through and the negotiations you brilliantly maneuvered are a testament to your dedication to your authors. I can't imagine there having been a better woman out there to lead me through this journey.

To my new and already treasured friend Amy Conway-Hatcher for penning a most beautifully elegant Foreward. Your vulnerable sharing of your personal experience, woven into your heartful appreciation for my offering within the pages of this book touched my heart ever-so-deeply.

To my mentor, come friend Adam Markel, who never made space for me to let myself off the hook when the ideas got scrambled and the words wouldn't come. Without your stabilizing presence this book would not have gotten written.

Charlotte Koppin, you will always have my sincerest gratitude and appreciation for rushing in at the 11th hour, with your tech genius and amazing team, to rescue this team and this project from the website weeds and the quicksand into which we had waded.

To my longtime friend Dr. Richard Kaye, I am deeply grateful for your multiple levels of support during this book's inception. I still remember the light switching on in your eyes as you exclaimed over a half-eaten lunch, "I know just the person you need to meet," while grabbing your phone to dash out a text that would change my reality.

With respect, admiration and love to the amazing women who contributed their words of wisdom to the chapters in this book...

Thank you, Annabel Ascher, for expressing the courage to share a story so well known to vast numbers of women, who rarely speak it out loud. Thank you for knowing that when one of us speaks a secret of how poorly we view ourselves, we no longer feel like 'the only' insufficient one. That moment of illumination grants us each permission to see ourselves through fresh eyes.

Sandra Bargman, what can I say? You are my friend, my sister, my sounding board, and you honor me with the space to be the same for you. Thank you for your constant emotional support through this process. The deliciously edgy words of vulnerability and mettle you candidly shared within this book are touching and poignant.

Janine Hamner-Holman, you are absolutely one of the most audaciously fabulous women I've had the privilege of calling 'friend.' Your belief in this book and my ability to produce it were a much-appreciated salve in my moments of becoming unwound. The insights you shared on workplace incivility between women are powerfully spot on and so essential to our times.

Thank you, Jane Bradley, for your ongoing support that has been presented in myriad forms. It is an amazing gift to have a friend and ally who has walked through the top echelons of the business world since decades before it was traditional for women. Thank you for shattering glass ceilings for all of us and for mentoring other women, including myself, to be able to reach our own greatest heights. And, thank you for all the great lunch conversations that never fail to take my mind off of the more harried moments and entertain!

Darling Shelly, (Dr. Shelly Gruenig) you are such a force for good! Thank you for sharing your story of opening the fascinating world of STEM to all the kids you impact by bringing it right into their neighborhoods and for helping them build faith in themselves by becoming the #1 ranked team internationally, led by (you) the #4 ranked STEM coach, worldwide. Most of all, thank you for being a treasured friend.

My dear Anne Sermons Gillis, you have been a friend and ever-so-amazing woman that I've looked up to for over 30 years. Your decades of traveling the world in advocacy for women has continuously inspired me and so many others. I remain honored that you agreed to contribute your wisdom to this book.

Thank you, Karen Boise, for sharing your first-hand knowledge of the coaching world. As is well documented, this is an arena where women are often hesitant to tread. Your insights will surely help some to take that leap, to their own betterment.

Jackie Nagle, the minute I met you I knew I was speaking with a woman of brilliance, compassion, insight and fabulous wit! It is a joy to have you in this circle. The information you shared is profound in revealing the disparities of how women from different races and cultures are treated from each other. It has touched me deeply and expanded my understanding of the equity imbalances in our workplace culture. I am immensely grateful to you for jumping in to contribute to this book.

To my invaluable editing team...

All writers need an editor. I needed an entire team.

Thank you Annabel Ascher. Your contribution was vital in helping me untangle my mind and ideas so they could begin to take on a structure that made sense.

To Sara Diehl, you are an absolute delight to work with and to know as a mighty woman. From copywriting, to making the book proposal make sense, to jumping in and helping with the marketing copy, and more, you were all in from the moment we met. I am truly grateful to you for every contribution.

My dear friends, Karen Kuhl and Sarah Maes. Being able to lean into you both to do late-date read throughs was invaluable to the book and even more so, my peace of mind.

You are all amazing and I am most grateful to and for each of you. Thank you for each bringing your different and unique styles to this book. I can see your individual fingerprints throughout and every one of them makes the book better than it would have been without any single one of you.

To the amazing and cleverly creative members of our little TEAMLESLEY, without whom I'd be lost on a daily basis...

Thank you my dear Makenzie Gruenig for expressing your exceptional skill with videography, editing and in general making me look better than I otherwise might. Laurin Sauls your attentive commitment to my social media presence has been invaluable, as has been your seemingly endless patience with my non-techy brain. Lex Lyford, without your tech genius I'd be regularly out of the game. Vida Antonijevic, your astute attention to the administrative tasks so numerous that they were depriving me of time to write has been a breath of fresh air. Thank you Emily Hook for your attention to my website and podcast.

Isa Cocallas, you have my steadfast gratitude for keeping this train on its tracks and regularly running ahead to lay new track. From graphic design on smaller projects, to my beautiful book cover, to design support on the website, to guiding and supporting every individual on the team to discover their personal best, to what has become a valued friendship, I will be forever grateful for our having encountered each other.

My cheerleaders of a lifetime

To my beloved sister, Carol Ann Jerome, even when we were just kids you were wise beyond your years and now, all these years later, you are the wisest mighty women I know. Like a north star, thank you for being my constant in so many ways.

To my person, Rosalie Grace, you are the most loyal, encouraging, funny friend a woman could want, not to mention a great travel companion and playmate. You've been a rock. I cherish you dearly.

To my dear friends who have always had my back, cheered me on, trusted me with their most cherished secrets and joined me in juicy, delicious laughter...

Steve Fuhlendorf, Angela Legh, Kamila Chlebkova, Ellary Simms, Sarah Berger, Angelika Koch, Skip Walsh, Brauna Brickman, Jennifer Donaldson, Kate Gonzalez, Marianne DiBlasi, Alaya Chadwick, Mindy Weschler, Dwight Miller, Charlet Pelissier, Beth Kennedy, Monai Reid, Anna Gonzales, Clare Williamson, Kristy Ross LaMariana, Vincent Rowe, Janie Corinne, Enoch Ortega, Gayle Dillon, Paul Dillon, Karin Lubin, Virginia Hall, Harriette King, Frances Salvato, and each of the 100's of women who have been friends, colleagues, champions and influences in my life throughout the years.

CPSIA information can be obtained
at www.ICGtesting.com
Printed in the USA
JSHW021300050722
27596JS00001B/45

9 781513 693781